THE PRIORITY OF LABOR

THE PRIORITY OF LABOR

A Commentary on *Laborem exercens*,
Encyclical Letter of Pope John Paul II

Gregory Baum

 PAULIST PRESS • *New York/Ramsey*

Library of Congress
Catalog Card Number: 82-81632

ISBN: 0-8091-2479-3

Published by Paulist Press
545 Island Road, Ramsey, N.J. 07446

Printed and bound in the
United States of America

Contents

COMMENTARY

Introduction

Pope John Paul II's encyclical, *Laborem exercens,* has lifted Catholic social teaching to a new height. The first Polish Pope in history, a citizen of the second world, brings to his task a special sensitivity and his own political experience. In the critical treatment of industrial society and its present crises he constantly looks in two directions—toward the communist countries of Eastern Europe and toward the capitalist societies of the West. In his encyclical he wants to find principles of social justice applicable to Eastern and Western societies and at the same time relevant to the third world. This is a daring undertaking. We shall see that while the encyclical remains in continuity with the Church's social teaching, it introduces new ideas, derived from a critical and creative dialogue with Marxism, which allow the author to reread the Catholic tradition in a new light and raise the Church's social message to an unprecedented height. We shall see throughout this commentary that Pope John Paul II permits himself to be impressed by certain Marxist insights. Yet in the discussion of these insights he opens them up, overcomes their rigidity, expands them toward new meaning, and thus produces a social philosophy that transcends Marxism from within.

This turn to a dialogue with Marxism comes as no surprise. The Polish Church has long been engaged in a struggle for freedom against the communist government identified with a determinist, atheistic version of Marxism. Among Polish Catholics there were two distinct approaches to Marxism, one which repudiated Marxism altogether and wanted nothing to do with it, and the other which was open to dialogue, appreciated certain positive elements, and tried to overcome the errors of Marxism with arguments drawn from Christian personalism.[1] Karol Wojtyla, the present Pope, formerly Archbishop of Cracow, was close to this second group. What is this Christian personalism? It is an approach to man in society, derived to a large extent from the French Catholic thinker, Emmanuel Mounier, founder of the review *Esprit*, which was critical both of capitalist individualism and Marxist collectivism. Against the individualists, personalism argued that the person was essentially social: a person came to be through collaboration with others. And against the Marxists, personalism argued that even in the joint effort to build society, people remained persons, subjects, bearers of an inner life of transcendent value. Especially after World War II, Emmanuel Mounier advocated a form of socialism, built on the social ownership of the industries, which recognized the inwardness and freedom of people not just as a concession to individualism but as an essential dimension of the joint socialist project. The personalism of *Esprit* was influential among a group of Polish Catholics. They wanted to correct and enrich Marxism with the help of personalist insights. This group was vehemently opposed by the intellectual circles close to the Polish government; it was also criticized by conservative Catholics, some of them in high places, who preferred the total repudiation of Marxism. Karol Wojtyla protected the personalist group.

Karol Wojtyla took this approach to the Chair of St. Peter. His early publications as Pope John Paul II revealed his critical opinion of Marxist thought. While the Pope repudiated the authoritarianism, the atheism and the bureaucratic rigidity of the communist countries, he was quite willing to draw upon socialist arguments to criticize the capitalist society of the West. In one place the Pope argued that the present capitalist system no longer sufficed to provide the world's population with the basic requirements of existence; what was needed was a carefully planned economy, one based on the cooperation of the nations.[2] In another place the Pope argued that workers in modern industrialized society have been "alienated" from the fruit of their labor: they have no share in the ownership of their products nor are they entitled to participate in the policy-making of their industries.[3] This line of thought drawn from Marx's writings is given a central position in the present encyclical. On several occasions the Pope has severely criticized "the consumerism" of modern

Western society. This word refers to the importance assigned in capitalism to commodities, to the comforts of life and the standard of living: capitalism creates a consciousness that evaluates human life in terms of private material satisfactions. A century earlier Marx had referred to this as "commodity fetishism." Marx had then argued that this form of materialism was inherent in capitalist production. It is no great surprise, therefore, that in the present encyclical Pope John Paul II engages in a critical and creative dialogue with Marxist thought.

The immediate occasion for writing the present encyclical was the ninetieth anniversary of *Rerum novarum,* Pope Leo XIII's social encyclical of 1891, the starting point for what is usually known as "papal social teaching." Drawing upon the social thought of progressive Catholic movements in the nineteenth century, often referred to as social Catholicism, Pope Leo XIII initiated a social philosophy that was open to the modern world, criticized secularization and economic injustices, and provided guidelines for the political involvements of Catholics in society. Subsequent Popes have developed this social teaching. To commemorate the fortieth anniversary of *Rerum novarum,* Pius XI published the encyclical *Quadragesimo anno* (1931) dealing with the economic crisis of the depression. Forty years later, Paul VI commemorated the anniversary with a special letter *Octogesima adveniens* (1971) addressed to Cardinal Roy, then president of the Vatican Secretariat for Justice and Peace, in which the Pope dealt with the social conditions of the time. This letter recognized the changes going on in the third world after the end of the colonial era and for the first time acknowledged socialism as a rational option for Catholics. This was new. *Octogesima adveniens* warned Catholics against forms of socialism committed to a total world view such as Marxism, but remained open to forms of socialism that were pluralistic and left room for the religious dimension. Since *Laborem exercens* places itself in the context created by *Octogesima adveniens,* it is important to recall at this point the evolution of the Church's teaching on socialism.[4]

For Leo XIII socialism was an atheistic and materialistic doctrine at odds with Christian faith. The Pope was also critical of capitalism, especially the laissez-faire capitalism of this day, because it had divided society into two classes, owners of industry and workers, and inflicted upon the workers inhuman conditions of life. Leo XIII thought that a strong government dedicated to the protection of the common good should contain and steer the economy of the nation, encourage the unionization of labor, and make laws to protect workers from exploitation. Pope Pius XI, writing during the great depression, offered a more extended critique of the capitalism of his day, which by that time had become largely dominated by trusts and monopolies. Capital, the Pope argued in his encyclical, has become concentrated in the hands of a small elite, so powerful that it controls the flow of money, fixes prices and rates of interest, and exercises a power over the economy that prevents national governments from protecting the well-being of their people. According to Pius XI, monopoly capitalism generates ever greater economic empires and leads to conflict between nations and eventually destructive war. He spoke of the new imperialism of money.[5] At the same time, Pius XI did not wholly condemn the capitalist system. He still believed that strong governments dedicated to the promotion of the common good could control the economy by adequate legislation, tame and restrain the capitalist system, protect workers and the poor by appropriate laws, and thus assume responsibility for the well-being of their people. Pius XI, moreover, endorsed the condemnation of socialism. He specified that his condemnation referred to the revolutionary socialism of Russia as well as the democratic socialism of the Western European socialist parties. The Pope recognized that the social policies of democratic socialism resembled the social policies advocated by Catholic reformists, yet he argued that socialism in any of its forms bears within it the seed of atheism and class war and hence remains dangerous even in its moderate, democratic form. Socialism in any of its forms was out of bounds for Catholics. It was only in the pontificate of John XXIII, especially in his encyclical *Pacem in terris,* that papal teaching took a more open approach to the socialist tradition.[6] Under appropriate historical circumstances, John XXIII argued, socialism evolves beyond its materialist and atheist errors and becomes for Catholics a significant partner in dialogue. In 1971, Paul VI repeated this argument.[7] In fact, Paul VI went further by acknowledging that there were indeed forms of socialism which were appropriate for Catholic participation.[8]

In the following commentary on *Laborem exercens* I wish to

clarify the encyclical's social teaching and situate it in the contemporary debate over social theory. The focus of the encyclical, as the title suggests, is on human labor. Man is defined as worker. Man creates his own history through labor. Man is the subject of labor, and through his labor is meant to become more fully subject of his world. Man's self-constitution through labor is a moral task. The Christian recognizes that God is graciously present to this task. From these reflections the encyclical draws a number of moral principles. The central one of these, summing up the Pope's central message, is the priority of labor over capital. Capital is meant to serve labor, which means serve the workers in the industry, the expansion of the industry and the entire laboring society. The violation of this principle in Western capitalism and in Eastern collectivism is the source of oppression and misery in society. The workers' struggle for justice must aim at a social system in which the priority of labor over capital is observed. This happens only through the introduction of the co-ownership of labor on the one hand, and of a responsibly planned economy on the other. The struggle for justice, carried on by the exploited joined in solidarity, must be supported by those who love justice, which includes the entire Church. Only through such a struggle will justice come into society. The encyclical examines the role of technology in human labor. It also shows that family life, national identity and religion serve man laboring in becoming fully the subject of his history. At the end of my commentary, I try to clarify precisely what kind of socialism *Laborem exercens* recommends.

One more word before we start. Since the encyclical constantly speaks of man, of his labor and his destiny without indicating that "man" is used generically and that "his" always includes "her," the papal message may have a slightly alienating effect at least on North American readers. However, in some contexts, and I believe in this one, it is important to retain the term "man" as a generic reference. Yet when this is done it is equally important for the reader to recall that "man" is always to be understood as referring to both men and women in the text and also in the commentary.

Let us now turn to the encyclical. At first Pope John Paul II tries to clarify the historical situation in which he addresses himself to Catholics and all people willing to listen. What is taking place at this time is not simply an economic crisis and the decline of culture;

there are also new, positive developments that offer a challenge to human society. The Pope thinks that we are "on the eve of new developments in technological, economic and political conditions" (n.1) that will influence the world of work and production no less than did the industrial revolution of the last century. We are experiencing the beginning of a second industrial revolution, based on new forms of advanced technology. Some writers have labeled this, misleadingly it seems to me, as "post-industrial society." How does the encyclical describe the present turning point? It speaks first of the introduction of automation and computer control in the sphere of industry and organization; then it mentions the increasing costs of energy and raw materials, the acknowledgement of the limits of nature and the discovery that wide sections of this nature have already been polluted; and finally it recognizes the emergence on the political scene of peoples who have previously been subjugated and who now demand their rightful place among the nations. These radical changes will demand a profound reorganization of the economy. The immediate consequences of this may be unemployment for millions of workers. The encyclical foresees that these changes will lead to a slowdown or even regression of the industrial development of Western nations, including the United States and Canada, accompanied by a decline of wealth and standard of living; at the same time, the same changes could allow millions of people, until now condemned to shameful and unworthy poverty, to gain access to greater economic development (n.1). This is the picture of the present situation, including decline and recovery.

What wisdom does the Church have to offer to people at this juncture of their economic history? The encyclical argues that it is not the Church's task to engage in the scientific task of analyzing the present trends and examining the possible consequences; at the same time, since social and economic change involves people, the Church has always held that it must address itself to these issues. It is the Church's task as guardian of man's dignity to examine the historical conditions of human life from the viewpoint of social justice (n.1).

Man as Laborer:
Man as Subject of Labor

The first sentence of *Laborem exercens* introduces a perception of human life and human nature that is new in ecclesiastical documents. Through labor, we are told, people must produce their daily bread, must advance their understanding of the universe and their technological control, must raise the cultural and human level of the community to which they belong and of which they are part. Man is thus defined through labor in this prefatory paragraph: "Only man is capable of work, and only man works, at the same time by work occupying his existence on earth. Thus work bears a particular mark of man and of humanity, the mark of a person operating within a community of persons. And this mark decides its interior characteristics: in a sense it constitutes its very nature." Man is a laboring animal. Man differs from other animals because he labors. The activity of animals to procure food and protection is not strictly speaking labor because it is not grounded in freedom and reason. Animals follow their instincts. Human beings alone freely engage themselves, following the device of their own reasoning, in creating the conditions of their survival, growth, and development. Man labors every day to build up his existence, to produce his world, to create his history. It is in this labor that man reveals his special dignity.

While the encyclical offers us a rational analysis of man's self-making through labor, it also presents a biblical argument drawn especially from Genesis (n.4). Man is created in the image of God and appointed to subdue the earth. Man as bearer of the divine image has dominion over the earth. Man is appointed to labor to transform the portion of the earth he inhabits, and to engage in conscious activity to explore the universe and put it to human use. The divine words recorded in Genesis never cease to be relevant: "They embrace equally the past ages of civilization and economy, as also the whole of modern reality and future phases of development, which are perhaps to some extent beginning to take shape, though for the most part they are still almost unknown to man and hidden from him" (n.4).

Man labors. Man must work to survive as a being with biological needs. But since work is an activity which demands cooperation, man must create an organization of labor, and in fact a community in which members speak the same language, develop common values, and produce symbols that sustain their cooperation. Labor is thus highly personal and at the same time wholly social (n.1). The others are present in my labor as cooperators, as teachers, as providing the conditions that make my labor possible, as helping me to fulfill my biological and social needs so that I may continue my labor. The encyclical says that by labor man "occupies his existence on earth" (n.1). Man makes his world; and by doing so man reveals who man is and simultaneously becomes more authentically human (n.3). Through labor man actualizes his as yet unfulfilled potentialities. In the pursuit of the divine call, man in a certain sense creates himself.

Because labor is the axis of human self-making, it is also by labor that people are most vulnerable to wounds and distortions. Labor "contains the unceasing measure of toil and suffering, and also the harm and the injustice that penetrates society" (n.1). Disorder in the order of human labor is the principal cause of the injustices in society, the structures of oppression, and the alienation inflicted upon people. As we shall see, Pope John Paul II will argue that all the social problems of today's society in West and East are disorders connected with human labor: they are basically economic problems, problems that can be overcome only through the introduction of the right order of human laboring (n.3).

The encyclical defines human being through labor. This is not the only possible definition of humankind; the encyclical avoids all dogmatism at this point. Still, it is this definition of man as laborer that allows us to understand man's position in history, to analyze the threats to human being in present day society, and to move toward the construction of a society in which people are able to live more authentically human lives. Among many possible definitions of man, the Pope chooses this one for reasons of its historical usefulness and its transformative power.

Where does this perception of man come from? In the encyclical it is derived first of all from Scripture (n.4). Genesis speaks of man as created in the image and likeness of God and as such appointed to subdue the earth. Man is created as worker, in fact as agricultural worker, as gardener, farmer, steward of the earth. Since these ancient texts of Scripture were written in a society that was largely agricultural, this definition of the human being is not surprising. Even many New Testament texts reflect the rural and small town world of workers. Jesus himself was a laborer. Yet the Christian theological tradition, nourished largely by classical Greek thought, following Plato and later Aristotle, did not pursue this approach to man as worker. What distinguished man from the animals was reason. The ancient Greek centers of culture were slave societies. Here labor was assigned to the slaves. Free men did not work. Their glory was the pursuit of the intellectual life and the governance of society. What defined man's essence here was rationality. Women were acknowledged as rational too, even though in a subordinate way. Women were believed to be so absorbed in giving birth and the processes of nature that they did not manifest the full meaning of humanity. This aristocratic tradition, which defined man as rational and assigned workers and women to a subordinate place, profoundly influenced Christian theology, even though the Scriptures honor work and workers. In the spiritual tradition of the Church, especially among the great men and women of prayer, labor continued to be respected. The Order of St. Benedict defined its ideal in terms of "ora et labora," "pray and work," reflecting the needs of the declining Roman Empire, the break-up of the slave economy, and the search for self-reliant communities in the country. But in the intellectual tradition of the Church the Greek heritage proved strongest. Man was understood as the image of God because he was rational. Man differed from animals by his reason.

Defining the human being in terms of labor, we note, presupposes rationality. People work not by following their instinct as do animals, but by recognizing their needs, inventing a project that might meet their needs, and choosing the means adequate for the realization of the project. Work here presupposes reason, at least a certain kind of reason, one that is shared by the community and enters into its self-constitution through labor. This rationality is not simply a given; it grows and transforms itself precisely as people create new conditions for their communal existence, deal with new experiences, and rely on new forms of cooperation.

What is the direct source of the encyclical's definition of man as laborer? Such a definition was foreign to aristocratic society. It was equally foreign to the European societies created by the rising bourgeoisie in the eighteenth and nineteenth centuries. The European middle class, like the aristocracy, looked down upon labor and laborers. To do manual work was regarded as below the dignity of one's social position. The European middle class, unlike the emerging industrial class in America, developed manners and symbols that signified to the public that they did not have to labor. Middle class women especially were put into the kind of clothes that revealed to everyone that they did not do manual work. The philosophers attached to this society could not possibly draw from the laboring classes the metaphor of human self-understanding. It was Karl Marx, critic of bourgeois society, who introduced man's self-definition through labor into European philosophy.

Deeply disturbed by what capitalist industrialization was doing to working people, Marx tried to analyze society and its historical development by identifying with the workers and looking upon the social reality from their point of view. In his early writings produced in the 1840's, Marx defined man as worker.[9] Man differs from animals through labor. Man creates the conditions of his survival by work. This means that man must procure his bread by labor, i.e., produce the instrument and the social organization necessary for the transformation of that portion of nature which he can occupy, feed himself and create a dwelling. And by applying his rationality in this manner, man also creates his consciousness. Since work is by its nature communal, and since an economic system is meant to feed, house and protect the working people, the capitalist system, Marx argued, was in fact irrational. The bourgoise entertained an abstract form of reasoning that could not recognize the irrationality of the system. But the rationality of the workers, shaped by the social or collective nature of industrial labor, recognized the contradictions implicit in private ownership of the industries and hence in capitalism. Marx vehemently argued against an abstract definition of man as rational substance or soul. Such a definition made people blind to the reality known to all laborers, that till the end of time man must create his life by labor.

Pope John Paul II follows in the direction indicated by Marx. He does so because he believes that the understanding of man as worker corresponds to the letter and the spirit of Scripture, especially the Book of Genesis. At the same time, the Pope significantly expands Marx's notion of labor and, as we shall see, moves far beyond a Marxist anthropology. In the first place, the encyclical clearly indicates that labor does not refer principally to industrial labor as it tends to do in Marxist literature, but includes agricultural, clerical, scientific, service-oriented and intellectual work (nn.1, 4). Work includes homemaking in the family, services offered to society on all levels, as well as the governmental and managerial skills involved in the organization of production and the moderation of society. While the primary image of labor and the laborer is taken from the working class, it is applied to practically all members of society. All members make their contribution to the building up of society. The Pope does not recognize a place for a leisure class. Marginalized people and the unemployed, those who are not integrated into society, are meant to be workers; they are meant to share in the process of production and to make their contribution to the building up of the whole. Contemporary society is a laboring society. And because all people share in production, or at least are intended to do so, they all deserve to be remunerated by society in accordance with the norms of justice.

To expand further the notion of labor, the encyclical distinguishes between the *objective* and the *subjective* side of labor (nn.5–6). The *objective* side refers to the product of labor (n.5). This objective side then signifies the goods produced by industrial workers, yet because of the widened definition of work, it also includes the machinery of production and the technology operative within it, as well as the entire societal structure with the many-leveled services that keep production and society going. The encyclical, therefore, does not recognize the distinction, often found in Marxist literature, between productive labor, which produced goods, and non-productive labor, which serves industrial production more remotely and is therefore derivative and less significant for the creation of wealth. The wider definition of labor offered by the encyclical overcomes the classical Marxist view that the industrial proletariat is the single wealth-producing class and as such the singular organ of social reconstruction. The Pope argues, in this connection and in many others, that in today's world the industries have become interdependent, that they depend on the cooperation of all the sectors of society, and that in this advanced stage of industrialization practically the whole of society must be regarded as laboring, as productive, as participating in the wealth-producing process.

What is meant by the *subjective* side of labor? The encyclical defines the subjective side of labor as the transformation experienced by the laboring person (n.6). In the light of biblical revelation, the person who labors is following his vocation. God has created people to be creators and exercise their dominion over the earth for the well-being of all. Through work, then, man actualizes himself; man becomes the one he is meant to be. Even in the light of purely rational, secular reflection, man appears as one who becomes truly himself through his work. For in work a person expresses himself, assumes responsibility for his world, and prepares his own and society's future. It is through work, especially when understood in the wide sense employed in the encyclical, that people build their society as object; and through the same work they also become actors in history, responsible agents, creative persons, and thus collectively the subject of their own history (n.6).

The encyclical puts great stress on the subjective dimension of labor. Here lies its originality. Because through work people constitute themselves as subjects of their own lives and collectively of their common history, the subjective side of work holds primacy over the objective side. What happens to the subject of work is more important than what this work produces. The dignity and honor which work communicates to people is derived not so much from the objective dimension, from their achievement, from the product of their hands and minds, as from the subjective dimension; it is ultimately man's engagement which counts, his fidelity to the call, his increasing sense of responsibility, his self-realization (n.6). In labor the transformation experienced by the subject is of greater value and importance than the object produced. "The preeminence of the subjective meaning of work over the objective one" (n.6) is a principle that plays an important part in the reasoning of the entire encyclical.

This emphasis on the subject is a personalist position drawn from Pope John Paul's philosophical background. Karol Wojtyla had developed a philosophical approach, inspired by the French personalist Emmanuel Mounier, and by German phenomenologists such as Max Scheler, which put primary emphasis on subjectivity, i.e., on man's entry into personhood through fidelity and other self-actualizing commitments. The Polish thinker believed that this approach would enrich and expand the Catholic philosophical tradition. In a previous paragraph we noted that Archbishop Wojtyla stood close to Polish Catholics who believed that this personalist approach would also enrich and thus significantly modify Marxist thought.

The emphasis of *Laborem exercens* on the subject of labor is the application of the personalist principle to the understanding of man as laborer. This emphasis is certainly in keeping with the Christian tradition. In Christian preaching, the special dignity of the worker has always been derived from his personal engagement, fidelity and dedication, and not so much from the value attributed by society to the work done. Even workers engaged in menial tasks are deserving of honor; their dignity is that of faithful servants.

The emphasis on the subject of labor is not at odds with Marx's original social philosophy. In his early writings especially, Marx greatly stressed the subjective side of human labor. Marx argued that workers are meant to be responsible for their work, that they are meant to be the subject of their work and not disappear in the process of production as objects.[10] Marx analyzed the conditions of production that prevent workers from being subjects, that remove responsibility and creativity from them. According to his analysis, the objective side of labor, the product, the machinery, the industrial process has been allowed to take over and become the all-important thing. The owners and managers of the industries tend to look upon workers not as subjects but as objects, as part of the material factors that enter into the productive process. And because they are regarded as objects and treated as objects, workers easily experience themselves as objects. They lose the sense that they are subjects, or at least meant to be subject. This, Marx argues, is one aspect of the alienation of labor. The reason why industrial production alienates workers from their human substance is that in capitalism the industrial machinery is privately owned; and from this it follows first that the goods produced by the workers do not belong to them but to the owners of the machinery, and, second, that the conditions of production are not determined by the people who actually do the work but by the owners and their managers. As we shall see, Pope John Paul II shares some of these critical reflections. He too will argue that justice in society can be established only when workers become co-owners and co-policymakers in their industries.

In his early writings, Marx did not confine his analysis of alienation to the workplace. He argued more widely that people are meant to be the subject of their own society, and of all the institutions to which they belong.[11] People are meant to participate in the decisions that affect their common lives. People are to be the subject of their own history. The powerful forces in society that prevent people from exercising this co-responsibility and thus from being the subject of their society are the sources of human alienation. And since it is man's high destiny to be subject, it is his human task to wrestle against the alienating powers and assume collective responsibility for his work and its future.

In his later writings, Marx pays little attention to man as subject of labor and subject of history. Scholars do not agree whether the mature Marx changed his mind.[12] Did he move away from the emphasis on the subject, concentrate exclusively on the system of production and its laws, and develop a determinist theory of history? Or did he keep his concern for the worker as subject, analyze the system of production as principal source of human alienation, and retain the vision of workers struggling to become subjects of their history? In any case, in the official Marxism of the Soviet bloc countries, the concerns of the young Marx have been largely forgotten. The attempt to revive the attention to the subject, whether this be done by Marxists or by Christians, is regarded in these countries as unsettling and subversive.

While Pope John Paul II recognizes the alienation of labor and, as we shall see, attributed it to the distortions in the system of production, his main emphasis is not on alienation but on the fact that despite alienation man remains the subject of work (n.6). Subjectivity cannot be taken away from the worker. Even if a system of production assimilates workers as objects, they remain inwardly alive; they remain capable of criticizing the conditions of labor, of organizing themselves against these conditions, and of struggling for a more just economic system. The encyclical strongly emphasizes that the subjective dimension of labor never wholly disappears; the worker, man, remains subject. Man's subjectivity, made in the image of God, cannot be taken away from him.

Man remains subject even under conditions of alienation. This is the principle that, in the perspective of the encyclical, assures the openness of human history to social change. Human subjectivity is the locus of the divine presence. That man remains subject even under the conditions of alienation is, moreover, an argument against a particular communist or Leninist theory. Communists have often argued that in capitalist countries the alienation of labor has so weakened the working class and so beclouded their self-understanding that there is need of a disciplined avant-garde political party that has a scientific knowledge of society and understands better than the workers themselves what is in their collective interest. This avant-garde party should then infiltrate working class organizations to assume their leadership. The theory of alienation is here used to justify deception and domination. Against this view of alienation, the encyclical argues that even under conditions of oppression man remains subject, summoned to responsibility.

Catholic readers may find the encyclical's vocabulary, especially the reference to object and subject, a little surprising. In the classical philosophical tradition assimilated in our theologies, we tended to look upon the world as a given; the world was object, and this included the people who made it up. We understood ourselves as part of objective reality. To come to know this world and these objects, the mind had to conform itself to this objective reality. Truth was defined as the conformity of the mind to the objective reality. Truth was objective. Indeed in this context, we regarded the subjective as the purely personal and idiosyncratic. The subjective was regarded as an obstacle to truth and hence had to be minimized as much as possible in the process of knowing. Similarly we believed in an objective morality, in a set of principles implicit in human life as given, independent of subjective considerations. The good life was one in conformity with these objective norms. In this context, we readily spoke of the priority of the objective over the subjective.

In the encyclical, as I read it, we find ourselves in a different intellectual tradition, closer to Hegel and Marx than to Aristotle and St. Thomas, even though not necessarily at odds with the latter. Here the human world is not a given; it is in fact being produced by human labor. In creating their world as object, people actualize themselves, become more fully subjects and hence in some sense create themselves. If the objective world they build is damaged by contradictions and structures of oppression, then they become the authors of their own distorted consciousness. And the children born into this society will be socialized into this false self-understanding and to that extent become people alienated from their true humanity. People become truly human only by producing a truly human society. People are meant to be subjects; if they are born into a society that prevents them from being the subjects of their lives, then they must struggle to become subjects and reconstruct the social order and its institutions so that they may assume responsibility for themselves. In all this the guiding norm is always human subjectivity. Truth here stands for the participation of the mind in man's struggle to become more fully subject. And morality is measured by the fidelity to man's call to be subject. In this context it is not surprising to speak, as the encyclical does, of the priority of the subjective over the objective.

This emphasis on man as subject does not invalidate the traditional Catholic concern for objectivity. It is true, no doubt, that by regarding the world, including the social reality, as object and objective, Catholic theology projected a very static concept of society and unwittingly legitimated the existing order, the status quo. Seeing man as subject laboring to make his world offers a more dynamic understanding of society and hence facilitates social transformation. Still, with its language of objectivity, Catholic theology wanted to give expression to the givenness of reality, to God's creation first of all and more especially to God's creation of human being. Calling moral norms objective, theologians wanted to say that it transcended individuals and their private plans. Man's moral character, too, was a given. This "givenness" remains protected in the new approach. For this "givenness" is precisely that man is subject and that any effort on his part to escape this destiny leads to destructive consequences. Any institution that prevents people from becoming the subjects of their lives sins against this "givenness," and hence against human morality.

The theological anthropology implicit in *Laborem exercens* is that man is created by God as subject and that man is called to actualize himself through labor. People create their society and thus in some sense constitute themselves. Human beings must labor to become who they are meant to be. Since people are sinners and construct for themselves a sinful world, they damage themselves (as subjects) and create prisons for themselves (as objects) which prevent them from being subjects in the full sense. The Christian message proclaims that God is redemptively at work in present history. God graciously summons people to struggle against the powers that damage their humanity. Thanks to this divine presence, it is possible to speak of man becoming the subject of his history and thus of man's making of man.

In the original Marxism, man was also recognized as subject. The entire meaning of history was man's struggle to become fully subject of his collective existence. The purpose of revolution was to enable people to become the subjects of their history. But because the subject character of the human being was not grounded on a metaphysical principle and because it was progressively weakened by a positivistic, evolutionary understanding of history, it tended to be forgotten and eventually disappeared altogether in the objective process of production. Man simply became an ensemble of social relations. Man was defined positivistically by the forces of production and the social relations determined by these. In the Marxist tradition, only the great critical figures, the thinkers who returned to the dialectics of Marx himself, have recalled human subjectivity and tried to assure a place for it in Marxist theory and practice.[13]

The primacy of the subject in the encyclical, we note, is not an existentialist principle. It in no sense promotes individualism. Pope John Paul's personalism does not encourage us to think of people as free individuals who decide to join in the building of a just society. In the perspective of the encyclical, people caught in alienation create their freedom precisely by laboring together in the joint project of building their world. A person needs others to become truly subject.

It is by working together, constructing, organizing, planning, by jointly building the world that people are faithful to their subjectivity and thus actualize their true nature. For the encyclical, freedom is social and therefore ultimately indivisible. We cannot be free if others are still oppressed.

The encyclical is not totally clear on all aspects of man's self-constitution through labor. The papal document recognizes of course that people promote human life in many other ways than by working; it mentions in particular love and the family, the search for national identity, and religion. Yet these fields of human engagement, as we shall see further on, are seen by the encyclical as serving man's labor, and especially as sustaining the subjective side of labor. One might refer to man's involvement in the family, the nation and religion as "social labor" and argue that this social labor must serve the productive labor analyzed in the encyclical. What remains unclear in the papal document, however, is whether the struggle for justice and hence political involvement is part of laboring. Since the encyclical includes governing society in the definition of labor, and since it looks upon the workers' struggle for justice as serving labor—we shall see further on what this means—I am inclined to argue that when the encyclical speaks of man making his world through labor, it includes the struggle for justice.

Let me also add at this point that Pope John Paul II does not reply to the difficulties raised by some political philosophers against the definition of man as worker. Is work really the appropriate mode of man's self-actualization? Are there not some signs that in the future there may not be enough work for everyone? Society may have to create a division of labor that allows people to work part-time and spend their energies on other activities. Is there not a disadvantage in defining man as worker? Does this not make it more difficult for people excluded from work to create their identity and live out of as yet hidden resources of their personalities? The encyclical is unperturbed by these questions. As we shall see, it greatly emphasizes full employment as a requirement of justice.

Before turning to the next topic, I must observe that "the pre-eminence of the subject" becomes for Pope John Paul an important critical principle that he applies again and again to liberate certain sociological concepts of their excessive objectivity. It is a common human tendency, often reinforced by the social sciences, to regard society as an object, a complex machine, a thing—in other words, to "reify" it. Personalist philosophy insists that societies are in fact people doing things together. It is possible to wish to "dereify" social structures in order to dissolve the concept of society altogether and deny the impact of social structures on personal consciousness and personal action. This, however, is not the "dereification" we find in the encyclical.[14] Pope John Paul tries to "dereify" certain concepts such as work force and working class in order to gain a better understanding of what actually goes on in society and how subjectivity is involved in the transformation of social structures. He argues, for instance, that to speak of the work force, as liberal economists easily do, is an unhappy reification because it causes managers to forget that work is actually done by people and to devise social policies that treat people simply as objects. As we shall see, the encyclical also dereifies the notion of working class; again in this class we have to do with people, and if they are to recognize their common condition, organize and struggle for justice, then this will only be because of their subjectivity.

The Priority of
Labor over Capital

The preceding reflections on labor and man laboring are not presented by the encyclical as a new theory designed to lead Catholics to a better understanding of the human reality. Defining man as laborer is not a theory in the classical sense. Pope John Paul argues, rather, that the urgent problems of this time, the oppressions taking place in Western societies, communist countries, and the regions of the third world, can be solved and overcome in practice only if we recognize man laboring as the central axis of human self-making and self-understanding. "Human labor is a key, probably the essential key, to the entire social question" (n.3). This reveals a new approach to theory. The truth about man is not sought as the answer to an abstract question, "What is human nature?" It is sought rather as the answer to the urgent historical crisis in which humans find themselves at this time. And if this answer is true, then it will in fact disclose the human condition to us in such a way that we can transform it and overcome the crisis. Truth here is the mind's participation in man's entry into humanization. In the language adopted by many contemporary theologians, truth is here perceived as the noetic dimension of praxis.

What is the central conflict which causes oppression, alienation, wars, and dehumanization in our time? Pope John Paul argues that in the industrial age, which is not yet completed, it is the conflict between capital and labor, i.e., between the small but highly influential group of entrepreneurs, owners and holders of the means of production, and the broader multitude of people who lack these means and who share in the process of production solely by their labor (n.11). The conflict about labor and laboring is the central problem of societies, be they in the West, the East or the third world; human life constitutes itself everywhere on the economic base. How did the conflict between capital and labor originate? Here is the encyclical's preliminary answer: "The conflict originated in the fact that the workers put their powers at the disposal of the entrepreneurs, and these, following the principle of maximum profit, tried to establish the lowest possible wages for the work done by the employees. In addition there were other elements of exploitation connected with the lack of safety at work and of safeguards regarding the health and living conditions of the workers and their families" (n.11).

We notice that according to the encyclical the present crisis is not due to sin or human selfishness in general. It is true that we are a sinful society, but this alone is no key to an understanding of the injustices under which people are made to suffer. Nor can the present conflict be understood in terms of rising nationalism and the conflicts between nations. It is not simply the struggle of empires for world domination. According to the encyclical, the conflict between capital and labor stands at the center of modern history, and the other conflicts and structures of oppression must be understood in the light of the economic infrastructure. Eventually the encyclical will have more to say about the history of capitalism. For the moment we must gain a better understanding of what capital is.

What is capital? First the answer is given in objective terms. Capital refers to the natural resources placed at man's disposal and the whole collection of means by which man appropriates natural resources and transforms them in accordance with his needs. Capital refers to the means of production, to the available raw materials, and the funds necessary to pay the workers and expand the technology. Yet if we look more closely at capital and "dereify" the concept, then we see that capital is "the result of the heritage of human labor" (n.12). The raw materials, while being part of nature and as such the gifts of the Creator, have been made available for production by labor, especially by labor in the extractive industries. The means of production, from the simplest to the most modern and sophisticated technology, have been designed and produced by people's labor. The funds necessary to operate the industry and to expand its technology are the result of labor, saved up over the years. "Everything that is at the service of work, everything that in the present state of technology (machines, factories, laboratories, computers) constitutes its ever more highly perfected 'instrument,' is the result of work" (n.12). Capital, even in its most colossal form, is the result of labor and bears the mark of human labor. When we "dereify" capital we find that it is actually labor, stored up labor. However complex, gigantic and automated the means of production may be, it is labor and labor upon labor.

Capital is labor that has become instrument. Following the personalist perspective, the encyclical insists that however complex, developed, and computer-guided the industrial machinery may be, it is man who remains the subject of work (n.12). It is man who constructs technology, controls it, supervises its operations, repairs it when it breaks down, and programs it in accordance with his purposes. Capital remains object; it can never be subject. The subject of industrial production is working people, including industrial laborers and workers engaged in clerical, managerial, scientific and service occupations. And since in today's society industrial production is interconnected and involves the whole of society (connecting industries, transport, communication, legal system, schools for training workers, universities, etc.) it is really the laboring society that is "the real, efficient subject" (n.12) of work. The encyclical argues that capital is in the last analysis only a collection of things. Primacy in the productive process must be given to the subject. Capital, production and labor are united in the identical subject.

This argument leads the encyclical to a very radical position. The idea that capital is stored up labor is found already in the liberal economists of the eighteenth century. In fact, Marx quotes them when he adopts the same formula.[15] But while the liberal economists found no contradiction in capitalism, Marx argued that since capital is just the accumulation of labor, it really belongs to the laborers who produced it. The capitalist owns the productive machinery, but even this has been produced by laborers and therefore belongs to them. The private ownership of capital, Marx argued, is therefore theft.

The encyclical while radical in its own way, does not move in this direction. There are several reasons for this. One of them is that the crucial question in regard to capital is not its *ownership* but its *use.* How is capital used? Pope John Paul II comes to a more dynamic answer than Marx. Let us follow this argument.

The encyclical argues that since capital is accumulated labor, it cannot be separated from labor; it is united to labor. The opposition between capital and labor that has occurred in history is a contradiction. What does it mean to speak of "the unity of capital and labor"? Both are united in the subject of labor. However dispersed capital, machinery, raw materials, and labor may be as objects, they are united in their subject, which is man laboring, and in today's world, the laboring society. We have here an application of the personalist principle of the primacy of the subject. Since the intrinsic unity of capital and labor must not be violated, capital must be used to serve labor. The "ownership question" is not as important as the "use question." That capital must serve labor is the major principle formulated by the encyclical, and it is referred to as "the priority of labor over capital" (nn.12–13). In the following we shall examine more carefully what this radical principle means.

The first question we must ask is why labor and capital have come to be opposed to one another. Why has the priority of labor over capital been violated in the industrial age? The Pope speaks here of a distorted economics. He argues that in the early days of industrialization, the economists came to look upon labor and capital as distinct, separate and oppositional quantities operative in the productive process, whose interrelation could be determined by scientific means. Why? Because the behavior of workers followed the laws of the market. The human being was here looked upon as an economic unit. Human behavior was determined and predictable because it followed the laws of economics. This error, which the encyclical calls "economism," is a form of materialism (n.13). The capitalist class and the liberal economists promoted a "practical materialism" (n. 13). While they did not deny spiritual reality in theory, they presupposed that in actual fact the human person acted in accordance with economic laws. This false practice, the encyclical continues, eventually gave rise to a false theory, "theoretical materialism" (n. 13), which denied spiritual reality altogether. While Marxism protested against the subordination of labor to capital, i.e., the subjugation of the workers to the profit-making of the industrialists, it retained and endorsed the error of economism. Marxism continued to understand man largely in economic terms, explained culture and consciousness as a reflection of the economic conditions, and denied the reality of the spiritual. The encyclical designates this position as "dialectical materialism."

While Marxism looked upon man as an economic creature, it came to quite different conclusions than did the liberal economists. In Marxism, economic interests determined not only the material behavior of people—that is what the liberal economists held too—but also the form of culture and the orientation of consciousness. At the same time, Marxism seemed to argue that through the raising of consciousness it was possible for workers to discover their collective plight, their subservience to the market, recognize that as the producers of wealth they had power, and organize a labor movement to change the economic system and advance their collective self-interest. Through the raising of consciousness, workers could become united as a class. What is this "raising of consciousness"? Is this a spiritual process embodying personal intelligence and freedom? Or is this a necessary process, defined by the economic factors of the conditions of labor, which can be predicted scientifically? The encyclical interprets Marxism as an economic determinism, as a scientific interpretation of history, which explains human life in positivistic terms. The official Marxism of Eastern Europe presents itself precisely in this deterministic, economistic, anti-spiritual, and atheistic manner.

It is important to point out, however, that it is also possible to give a spiritual interpretation of this "raising of consciousness" through which people recognize their alienation, distance themselves from an individualistic self-understanding, and join in solidarity to form a class struggling for its rights. In the Eastern European countries but more especially in Western societies, there are many revisionist Marxists who accept the creativity of consciousness, repudiate economic determinism, and understand the class struggle as the historical destiny of people to become free subjects of their own history.[16] These revisionist Marxists argue rather convincingly that they represent Marx's own social philosophy. While the process of production is indeed the primary axis of man's self-making, the transition from one system of production to another takes place through the creativity of human consciousness. Man's freedom is here involved. These authors call their position, which they equate with that of Marx himself, "dialectical materialism," while they designate the determinist, official Marxism as "vulgar Marxism." (The encyclical does not follow this vocabulary.)

The reasoning of the encyclical is here of great interest. We are told that a certain practice, "practical materialism," preceded the theoretical position, in this case "theoretical materialism." Because men acted in a certain manner, they eventually came to think in a different way. In classical thought, we always believed that it happened the other way around. First came the idea, and then only the application. The perspective of the encyclical is different: it concedes primacy to practice. Pope John Paul II is here quite specific. He says that the economic theories of the liberal economists were historically rooted in the distorted practice of the early capitalists who hired laborers at the lowest market price and treated them as if they were purely economic units in the productive process, aimed at the maximization of profit. These early entrepreneurs, through actions that were both immoral and irrational, produced the separation of capital from labor. What Pope John Paul II must have in mind here is the decision of these entrepreneurs to break away from the feudal order, in which ownership—in feudal days mainly ownership of land—was associated with certain social duties, in particular with responsibility for the well-being of the serfs and peasants living on the land. The priority of labor over capital was violated in practice before it was justified by a theory. We shall return further on to the primary role of practice in the creation of ideas.

Finally we note that, according to the encyclical, there was nothing necessary in capital's opposition to labor. It was not the inevitable consequence of private ownership; it resulted rather from the choice of the early industrialists who, giving in to greed and stupidity, organized their capital against the workers. We have here again a "dereification" of an historical process. Responsible for history are ultimately people thinking and choosing.

The encyclical pursues a similar "dereification" of the historical class conflict. Pope John Paul II argues that the Marxist theory of the inevitable class conflict is an abstraction from the historical experience of people actually struggling against the owning class. We are told that the conflict between capitalists and workers in the early nineteenth century, provoked by the capitalists' exploitation of labor, eventually came to be interpreted as a conflict between two ideologies (n.11). Liberalism (in the European sense) came to be looked upon as the ideology of the capitalists; it defended the freedom of individuals to pursue their personal interests, the freedom of the market safe from government interference, and the role of the market as stimulus to production, as agency of distribution, and, following the law of supply and demand, as regulator of production and the distribution of goods and wealth. Marxism came to be looked upon as the ideology of the workers; it presented itself as representative of the worldwide proletariat and as key to the understanding of history. In both cases, the encyclical argues, the ideologies looked upon people as acting in accordance with fixed laws. Both ideologies were "reifications."

Let us see how the encyclical elaborates what this means in the case of Marxism: "The real conflict between labor and capital was transformed into a systematic class struggle, the terms of which could be determined scientifically, and the exercise of which included ideological and especially political means" (n.11). The Pope then briefly describes official Marxism: the class struggle, the victory of the proletariat, the collectivization of the means of production, the monopoly of power exercised by the workers' party, the elimination of class injustices and the overcoming of the classes themselves. Today the ideologists of this sort of Marxism understand their collectivist society as part of a broad international movement that will eventually introduce the communist system throughout the world. We have here a modest hint that Marxist ideology can serve as a theoretical defense of world domination. The same is also true of the ideology of individual freedom.

The encyclical offers a brilliant argument against the determinist understanding of the class struggle, the heart of the official Marxist philosophy. This argument, as we shall see, is an exercise in "dereification." It is an argument against Marxism, at least in its official version, even though it reasons from within the perspective of Marxism. So far the encyclical has recognized that people create their human world by labor and that in doing so they in some way create also themselves. The papal document has acknowledged that capital and labor belong together, that the opposition of capital to labor is essentially irrational and immoral, and that in today's world, marked by advanced industrialization, labor has become social, that is to say, that it involves not the few but the many, the great majority. For this reason, capital must serve the entire laboring community. Where the encyclical differs from Marxism is in the interpretation of class conflict.

Pope John Paul argues that the struggle of workers against the capitalist class was not due to historical necessity, nor to forces beyond their personal option; on the contrary, the workers' struggle for social justice came from the realization that they were oppressed, that singly, one by one, they could not improve their material situation, and that only in solidarity with all the workers in their situation would they be able to gain the power to reconstruct society in accordance with greater justice (n.8). Labor solidarity is not the work of necessity, but the result of consciousness, freedom and personal choice. Real people are involved in class conflict, people who reflect on their experiences, discuss their ideas with one another, establish bonds of solidarity, and learn to act together. According to the encyclical, it is the solidarity of the oppressed, which is ultimately a *moral* reality, that accounts for the struggle of the exploited against the powerful and the transformation of society in the direction of greater justice.

Pope John Paul II offers here an imaginative rethinking of class conflict. The initiative for the struggle resides in the persons who recognize their common objective situation and freely commit themselves to solidarity in a joint struggle. The Pope calls the oppressed and the poor of the world to enter into solidarity, and he summons Christians who do not belong to this class to support it in the spirit of solidarity (n.8). In this context, the encyclical puts great emphasis on the historic role of unions (n.20). The Pope thinks that in today's world many employees who do not think of themselves as working class may have to organize in unions and create a wider bond of solidarity. He mentions in particular people with highly specialized training who work under conditions of grave injustice or who find themselves without work altogether. "Class consciousness" then is not the necessary result created by the contradictions in the economic infrastructure, nor is it confined to the class of industrial laborers; instead "class consciousness" is a rational reaction to the objective conditions of oppression, generated by free persons who recognize their situation and opt for solidarity as the only way out of their common predicament. The dynamic of Western history, the struggle for greater justice in society, resides in the free engagement of the oppressed. This is what the Marxist theory of class conflict becomes once it has been dereified, i.e., after the application of the personalist principle. We add from a theological perspective that since freedom is a divine gift, the dynamic of history is here presented as the locus of God's presence.

In this context, it is important that we attend to the crucial word "justice." The term is taken from the Christian, not from the Marxist tradition. The struggle of workers for the reconstruction of society is conceived by the encyclical as an entry of society into greater justice. This is in keeping with traditional Church teaching. The aim of the workers' movement is not seen as the conquest of the ruling class, be they the owners-and-managers of the industries or the government agents who manage the publicly-owned industries. The struggle of the workers does not aim at the reconstruction of society for the benefit of the workers alone; the struggle is not a war. It is rather a struggle which, through the show and use of power, aims at reorganizing labor and redistributing power in accordance with greater justice. While it may not be easy to define in detail what this justice means, it is clear that it includes the access of all members of the laboring society to the wealth produced by it, at least to enough remuneration so that they and their families can live with dignity and in modest comfort. Justice also includes the right of the people who do the work to participate in the decisions regarding production, distribution and the use of capital. *Justice means that capital is made to serve labor.* Because the workers' struggle, rightly conducted, is not simply an expression of their collective self-interest but also and at the same time a quest for social justice, it behooves those who love justice to extend their solidarity to the workers and identify themselves with their struggle. In the perspective of the encyclical, the struggle of the oppressed belongs to the moral order. The key words here are solidarity and justice.

We may raise the question whether the notion of justice fits into Marxist theory. It is certainly foreign to the determinist version of Marxism officially taught in the Soviet bloc countries. It is foreign to Marxist thinkers who regard Marxism as a science; for them the language of ethics and justice is an appeal to sentiment and expresses an ideology protecting the existing order of exploitation. Instead they appeal to the workers' collective self-interest, which they regard as the necessary and predictable motivation, produced by the conditions of the economic infrastructure. There are, however, revisionist Marxist thinkers who clearly recognize the moral dimension of Marx's thought. Marx argued, for instance, that the goods produced belong to the workers who made them, and not to the owner of the tools employed. He argued, in other words, that capitalism is based on theft. The capital produced should belong to the workers. Wage labor is, simply speaking, exploitation. While we may not agree with Marx's reasoning at this point, we nonetheless recognize that his rational argument has a moral character. Reason, for Marx, was not confined to scientific or technological rationality used in the control of nature; reason also touched the properly human and moral order. In this case, wage labor was judged to be at odds with the order of reason and hence immoral. This dimension of practical reason, present in Marx's own thought, is overlooked and rejected in the determinist Marxist orthodoxies.

We have dealt at some length with Pope John Paul's critical treatment of the Marxist ideology that dominates the Soviet bloc countries. The "dereification" of this ideology has led to an original Catholic interpretation of the class struggle, one that permitted itself to be inspired by Marx's ideas but went beyond them, especially through the application of the personalist principle. We now turn to Pope John Paul's treatment of the other ideology, economic liberalism, which gave a reified expression of the capitalist viewpoint, and over against which Marxism defined itself.

Economic liberalism defends a highly individualistic understanding of man. Each man pursues his own individual goal. Each person is free, or at least meant to be free, to pursue his own interests. How can society survive if each follows his own advantage? How can the good of all be protected if all become egotists? According to economic liberalism it is the market that transforms the egotism of the many into the care for the common good. The market urges the production of goods and services, serves as a distributing agent for these, and regulates prices by competition. The market fulfills these functions according to the law of supply and demand, thus regulating the flow of wealth in society and the universal availability of goods and services. What counts, according to this ideology, is that no power interfere with the market, no government regulation, no political pressures, no religious taboos and no traditional value. The market free of such interference promotes the well-being of the whole society.

Economic liberalism is based on an economic understanding of the human being. The encyclical calls this "economism." The deterministic versions of Marxism, we saw above, also constitutes a form of economism. According to the liberal ideology, man constitutes an economic being, *homo oeconomicus,* and therefore behaves in a determined and predictable manner in accordance with a cost-benefit calculus. Liberal economics regards itself, therefore, as a science in the strict sense. Just as physics detects the laws governing the physical universe, so economics is able to discover the laws operative in the lives of men and women. Such an economic determinism of personal life, we note, does not necessarily deny the existence of spiritual values. What it does, however, is to regard these values as matters of sentiment, high culture or religion, with no relevance for man's day-to-day behavior. Values do not interfere with the economic laws. Economic liberalism is, therefore, not opposed to Christianity, even though it holds that religious faith has no influence upon economic life.

Catholic social teaching has always rejected economic liberalism. In this encyclical, Pope John Paul refers to the practice based on this ideology as "rigid capitalism." It is rigid in excluding political forces from the market economy. Church teaching has always repudiated the individualism and the materialism implicit in the liberal philosophy. It rejected liberalism because it refused to recognize the impact of spiritual values upon economic life. According to traditional Church teaching, the freedom of the market protects the power of the rich, the resourceful and the clever, and allows them to triumph over the poor, the modest and the simple. Catholic social teaching insisted that it is the task of government to promote and protect the common good and to defend the poor against exploitation.

Laborem exercens adds to this the deeper insight that liberalism is an ideology that leads to a "reified" understanding of society. The free market economy never really existed. There were always some political forces acting upon the economic system. There were always some value perspectives that influenced people's economic behavior. The encyclical describes how in the industrialized parts of nineteenth century Europe the harsh conditions under which workers were condemned to live produced a "great burst of solidarity" (n.8). This fully justified response created strong working class solidarity stretching even across national boundaries. These workers' struggles brought about great changes in society. They modified the free market system. Improvements were introduced in the conditions of labor, in the remuneration received, and sometimes even in the participation of workers in the control of production. What has developed in the West through these changes is a more restricted capitalism, "neo-capitalism" in the terminology of the encyclical, in which the market forces are balanced by other forces, political, social, and cultural. How does Pope John Paul II evaluate the Western neo-capitalist system?

The encyclical recognizes that contemporary Western society is no longer defined by the free market, even if the old liberalism is still used for ideological purposes. Government is in fact deeply involved in the economy. This takes place not only through legislation protecting workers, but also through tariffs and other measures designed to stimulate production and trade. Government has assumed the task of providing, or at least subsidizing, the net of communication and transportation needed for the production and distribution of goods. Contemporary governments have industrial policies: they try to steer the economy and encourage the production of certain goods over others through a variety of techniques such as tax benefits, subsidies, risk insurance, and so forth. Governments have often been willing, especially when pushed by organized labor and movements of social reform, to provide some welfare for people whom the market system has damaged and who are unable to profit from it.

The encyclical might have mentioned that this "neo-capitalism" or reform capitalism has been promoted and defended by a neo-liberal social philosophy, developed in the second part of the nineteenth century, which has exerted considerable influence since then. Neo-liberal theory argues that the vitality of industrial production and commerce depends on the stability of society and demands that all members of society participate in consumption. It is therefore out of their own enlightened self-interest that the owners and managers of the industries and the large commercial and financial establishments should favor social peace, which means removing the grave injustices from society and preventing the dependent sector of society from being overly frustrated. Wages, moreover, should be increased so that the workers themselves become customers and in this way stimulate the economy. Capitalism, therefore, calls for social reform.

According to the encyclical, however, these improvements of the free market system are not the only changes that have occurred in the economy. New developments have taken place in the organization of capital and the development of technology that have grave consequences for workers and create new conditions of exploitation. The encyclical offers here only a few hints. There are references to the multinational corporations which have gained such enormous power that national governments are prevented from guiding their national economy and protecting their people from exploitation. This complaint we already find in the writings of Pope Paul VI.[17] The international character of capitalism enables companies to move their production plants to places where labor is as yet unorganized and raw materials are cheap, thus causing sudden unemployment in the countries they leave. The encyclical alludes to the monopoly control of resources such as oil, which allows corporations to raise prices and increase their profit at will. This organizational growth is accompanied by an extraordinary development of technology, in fact the entry into wholly new computer and communication technology, which introduces automation into the process of production and makes large numbers of workers superfluous. The relative achievements of neo-capitalism, the encyclical argues, are being undermined and destroyed by these new developments (n.8).

If we look at the international picture, we see that the oppression of people in the second half of the twentieth century is on the whole worse than the oppression inflicted on the workers of the nineteenth century. "On the world level the development of civilization and of communication has made possible a more complete diagnosis of the living and working conditions of men globally, but it has also revealed other forms of injustices, much more extensive than those which in the last century stimulated unity between workers for particular solidarity in the working world" (n.8). Matters have become worse. This evaluation applies above all, the encyclical tells us, to the countries that are on the way toward industrialization and to those that have an economy that is largely agricultural. The encyclical here alludes to the phenomenon of underdevelopment, that is to say, to the oppressive conditions created by capitalist developments, controlled by corporations from the North Atlantic centers, taking place in the countries of Asia, Africa and Latin America, usually designated as the third world. Because the whole earth has become the hunting ground for the multinational corporations the social reforms associated with neo-capitalism are being undermined and at a point of being lost. While in reform capitalism capital was made to serve labor to a certain extent, the global picture today reveals that capital serves labor less and less. For this reason, the encyclical argues, we must expect a new "burst of solidarity" (n.8) and organized action among these groups and peoples who are oppressed by the existing order.

Allow me at this point to summarize what the papal teaching of the past has said about the capitalist system.[18] I mentioned above that Catholic social teaching has always repudiated the ideology of liberalism. The Church defended the traditional position that it is the function of government to promote and protect the common good. Government must intervene in the economic order to protect the helpless and establish norms that assure the human treatment of workers. At the same time Catholic teaching defended the right to private ownership of the industries and for this reason vehemently opposed socialist movements and socialist parties which denied this right to private property. To many social critics, the Catholic Church appeared here as the defender of the owning classes. It must be added, however, that while the Popes blessed the private ownership of capital, they insisted that the use of capital must be social. The use of capital must serve the common good; and to achieve this what was needed was strong government, situated above the class conflict in society, which regulated the economy, made laws protecting labor, and used the wealth produced to advance the well-being of the community. The distinction between "ownership" and "use" of capital was incomprehensible to people living in capitalist society. Even Catholics living in these lands found it difficult to understand this teaching. For in liberal societies, ownership is defined precisely in terms of the right to use or destroy as one wishes. In the Catholic tradition, ownership was always seen as being associated with certain duties. Property may indeed be private and hence passed on to one's heirs, but the use of this property was not private; it had to serve the common good. Ever since Pius XI's encyclical *Quadragesimo Anno* (1931), written during the great depression, papal teaching acknowledged the right of society to nationalize privately owned industries and financial institutions; this right could be invoked whenever these corporations had become so powerful that it had become impossible for government to protect the common good.[19] What the papal teaching envisaged, I believe, was a highly restrained reform capitalism, freed from the monopoly control of the big corporations, guided by government policies, hemmed in by labor legislation, and accompanied by welfare programs. The Catholic parties of Europe and Latin America wanted to follow this vision. They regarded themselves as a middle road between capitalism and socialism. Indeed, in comparison with countries inspired by a liberal social philosophy, the Catholic parties appeared progressive. They were nonetheless capitalist, and whenever it came to conflict situations they defended capitalist over socialist interests.

Pope John Paul II's new encyclical raises serious doubts about the social good of this reform capitalism. It suggests that in the present situation, taking into consideration the global picture, this reform capitalism will no longer do. It is unable to make capital serve labor. In a previous statement, Pope John Paul had already expressed his position on the matter.[20] The present economic order, he then proposed, is unable to assure the well-being of the great majority of the people on this globe. A weakness of the encyclical is the absence of a detailed analysis of this new global picture. For when the Pope makes his recommendations for the reconstruction of the economic system, he seems to return to the national picture, the effort to make capital serve labor in each nation, leaving aside the global power which capital has acquired. We shall see in the following how Pope John Paul II envisages the reconstruction of society.

Laborem exercens proves that the two opposing ideologies, official Marxism and economic liberalism, are both erroneous, are both forms of "economism," are both "reified" images of the concrete struggles between workers and those who control capital and as such distortions of these historical processes. These ideologies disguise the historical reality and hence prevent people from grasping their own concrete situation.

As the liberal ideology gives a false picture of what actually goes on in capitalist countries, so Marxism blinds people from seeing the economic reality of the communist countries. In a few incisive sentences Pope John Paul II shows that while the means of production are publicly owned in communist countries, it is not the public but government departments that plan and manage the economy. The control of the economy places extraordinary power into the hands of the government. What easily takes place in such situations is that the economy is planned to serve not the laboring people but the political ambitions of the government and the strengthening of its hold over the people. The encyclical says that an economic system which violates the priority of labor over capital, by whatever name it may designate itself, is in fact a form of capitalism (n.7). The implication is clear: The economy in the communist countries is not socialism but state capitalism.

The papal encyclical here fully supports the viewpoint of the Polish labor union "Solidarity." It recognizes that the solidarity of the oppressed struggling for greater justice is the dynamic element of history, and it presents the communist state in which workers are unable to participate in the making of industrial policy as a travesty of socialism. In the Polish context, Solidarity stands for socialism, that is to say, for an economic system that recognizes the priority of labor over capital.

In communism as in capitalism, capital does not serve labor. Both systems, each in its own way, violate the priority of labor over capital. Only through "class struggle," in the extended sense presented above, can these ills be overcome. But before we turn to the strategies recommended by Pope John Paul II, we must ask whether he also has something to say about third world countries. This is not his main concern in this encyclical. Since the great masses of people in some of these countries are dispossessed and marginalized, they are not workers at all, and one may well ask whether it is possible to apply to them the analytical approach of the encyclical. While the dispossessed are not workers, Pope John Paul regards them as potential

workers; they are destined to be workers, they are meant to participate in the building of their society, and the fact that they are excluded from this process is a grave injustice and against the order of
reason. The teaching of the encyclical therefore also applies to them.
When the Pope writes, "In order to achieve social justice in the various parts of the world, in the various countries and in the relationships between them, there is a need for ever new movements of
solidarity of the workers and with the workers" (n.8), he is also
thinking of the third world. There too "the poor" (n.8) must enter
into solidarity, struggle for justice, for the right to participate in society as workers and responsible actors. This teaching is undoubtedly a
support for the liberation movements in the third world.

It is worthwhile to point out how the encyclical's view of "the
poor" differs from the classical Marxist position. For Marx it was
the industrial working class, the so-called proletariat, that had an
historic role in the class struggle and the deliverance of society from
oppression. In the Europe of the nineteenth century the working
class was at one and the same time the class that produced the
wealth and the class that was most oppressed. Because they were
producers of wealth they actually had their hand on great power,
and because they were oppressed, they had the motivation to revolutionize society. This peculiar combination made them the "universal
class," the class on whose shoulders rested the entry of society into
the new age. Marx himself had little sympathy for marginal people,
the unemployable, who slept under bridges in Paris. He called them
"Lumpen," the German word for hoodlum. They were not producers of wealth, they had no power, they were not shaped by the disci-
pline of work, they had no historic role. But the truth is that the
masses of people in some third world countries are precisely the marginal, the dispossessed, the Lumpen, excluded from participation in
the process of production. In these countries, the industrial proletariat is quite small. Classical Marxism does not apply to such countries
at all. There are many important attempts in third world countries to
reinterpret Marxism as a social theory that recognizes the oppressed
as the bearers of revolution. These theories perform major surgery on
Marxism. They envisage the struggle of the poor, united by solidarity, as the dynamic element that can revolutionize society. These theories have something in common with the teaching of *Laborem*

exercens. What is special in the encyclical, however, is that the struggle of the oppressed is always a struggle for justice within limits defined by justice, not a class war aimed at conquest and the free exercise of power.

Since the encyclical has "dereified" the notion of class conflict, recovered its concrete historical context, and redefined it in terms of the freely endorsed solidarity of the oppressed in the struggle for justice, it is necessary in each country and each situation to clarify who are "the poor," the oppressed, the people who must stand together in solidarity. This may not always be easy to do. The encyclical only says very briefly: "This solidarity must be present whenever it is called for by the social degrading of the subject of work, by exploitation of the workers and by the growing areas of poverty and even hunger" (n.8). We notice, moreover, that by speaking of "the poor," Pope John Paul II follows the vocabulary of liberation theology and the ecclesiastical documents of the Latin American church. In the industrialized countries, "the poor" are mainly the workers. In the nineteenth century the poor were mainly the industrial workers, while in some countries today a critical analysis shows that "the poor" are constituted by sectors of the population that also include agricultural workers, workers belonging to socially despised races or ethnic groups, and working women. In the third world, "the poor" may be the illiterate masses who live in hunger and misery. Pope John Paul II follows the Latin American liberationist trend when he declares, "The Church is firmly committed to the cause of 'the poor' for it considers it to be its mission, its service, a proof of its fidelity to Christ, so that it can truly be the 'Church of the poor' " (n.8).

The call for the solidarity *of* the poor and *with* the poor is truly a radical Christian principle. It is materialist and spiritual at the same time. Allow me to point to two extraordinary applications of this principle. First, the solidarity with the poor provides a critical principle that remains operative even when the collective struggle for justice has been successful, even when a liberation movement has led to social revolution. This principle then demands that Christians turn their attention to those groups that remain in the margin after the reorganization of society. While Christians are called upon to identify themselves with movements of solidarity, and in the third world with liberation movements, they do this not in an idolatrous fashion by abandoning their own religious vision, but by bringing to the struggle a critical principle that serves as guide even during and after the victory. One would be hard-pressed to find a purely secular principle that reveals such transcendence.

Pope John Paul II's call to universal solidarity responds to another burning question: Why should workers in the industrialized countries wrestling for justice in their own societies be concerned about justice in the third world? Social theories that locate the motivation for social change simply in the collective self-interest of the workers (as in Marxism) or in the enlightened self-interest of the ruling class (as in neo-liberalism) are unable to provide cogent arguments why people of the developed countries should reach out in solidarity to the poor of the third world. Only religion or religiously based convictions can make the unity of humankind a felt reality and a motivating factor. We are responsible for one another before God. This question also poses itself very painfully in third world countries where labor unions struggling for greater justice for the working class must decide whether they should enter into solidarity with the great masses of the poor. A similar question, for which a purely secular social philosophy has no answer, is why the men and women who struggle for justice should take upon themselves so many hardships, even though they expect their movement to be successful only at a future time when they will be gone. Workers, oppressed people, and those in solidarity with them have made and are still making these sacrifices, but collective self-interest does not account for their motivation. Most of them do not ask why they take these burdens upon themselves. They feel it in their bones that they must wrestle for justice. Whether they realize it or not, their motivation is religious. Universal solidarity can only be based on faith—on a faith in man's promised destiny. In my mind, this is a materialistic argument for religion. In the most concrete, down to earth, bread-and-butter sense, God makes humanity possible.

The Struggle for Justice

After analyzing the manner in which the priority of labor over capital has been violated in capitalist and communist societies, the encyclical turns to solutions and indicates in what direction the struggle for justice must move. What is demanded is an effort on two fronts, one in the direction of decentralization and the other, in creative tension with the first, in the direction of centralized planning. Let us examine these two phases.

The first question that demands an answer is how the priority of labor can be assured. We have seen above that the nationalization of the means of production is by itself no guarantee that the priority of labor is respected. This is made abundantly clear in the communist countries where the economy is run in the interest of the government's political purposes. While socialists in Western society may bracket the communist experience in their minds and speak confidently of nationalizing the industries and the financial institutions, the Pope from Poland is unable to disregard the communist experience. While writing the encyclical, the Polish author always asks himself how each sentence and each paragraph will be heard in the communist world. And since it regards truth as operational, the encyclical does not want to formulate social policy in a way that, while having progressive meaning in the West, has reactionary meaning in the East. We mentioned above that, for this encyclical, truth does not confirm the existing order as object; rather truth is the manner in which the mind lays hold of the existing order and initiates its transformation. This is not an identity-concept of truth where truth protects the identity of what is, but a non-identity concept of truth where truth reveals the distance between what is and what ought to be and ushers in the appropriate transformation. To speak of the nationalization of the industries is non-identity language in the Western world and may indeed be progressive, but it would be identity language in the communist countries and only confirm their totalitarian structure. We shall see that by applying the personalist principle, Pope John Paul II shall redefine "the socialization" of the means of production in a way that is critical and progressive in both West and East.

The nationalization of industries in the West may be useful and in some circumstances even necessary, but in and by itself this move does not guarantee the priority of labor over capital. The only way in which this priority can be achieved and protected, the encyclical argues, is through the participation of workers in the direction of their industries (n.14). The technological workbench at which they labor must in some sense be their own (n.14). They must be responsible for it. Whether industries are owned by private companies or by the government, what is necessary is that workers become in some sense co-owners, achieve co-responsibility for production and the use of capital, and co-determine the policy of the industry.

While Pope John Paul II affirms the principle of co-determination in a categorical fashion, he is non-doctrinaire in regard to the degree and the manner in which co-determination is introduced in various societies. The encyclical is open to a gradual entry of workers into this collective responsibility. The Pope praises all experiments in joint ownership, workers co-shareholding, workers' participation in decision-making, representation of workers on policy boards, and so forth, whether these be undertaken in Western or Eastern societies (n.14). It is only through such a democratization of the workplace that the priority of labor over capital can be protected. The workers themselves, those who labor in the industries (and this includes not only the industrial workers but all engaged in the industry including management and scientific researchers), must be involved in the decisions that control the capital they produce and make it serve them as workers, serve the industrial production in which they are engaged, and serve the laboring society as a whole.

This principle of co-ownership and co-responsibility raises serious questions in regard to Western and Eastern societies. Democracy at the workplace is at odds with capitalist theory. Workers are hired simply for their labor power; they have no claim to the ownership of the goods they produce nor to responsibility for management. The cooperative movement, created in the 1840's, defined itself against the capitalist organization of labor. Advocating the cooperative ownership of the units of production by the workers who labored in them, the movement created an economic counter-culture in capitalist society. It was successful above all in organizing small producers, farmers and fishermen and creating retail stores and credit unions. Cooperatist theory argued that private ownership inevitably made people selfish because they had to think of their personal benefit in order to survive, and that wage labor in capitalist institutions made people passive and dependent, undermining their sense of self-responsibility. Capitalism therefore creates alienation on both sides of the great divide. Cooperative ownership, on the other hand, delivers people from wage labor and from egotism. Here the daily labor for bread and life calls for cooperation, concern for the others, and joint responsibility, and hence initiates people into an altruistic consciousness.

Wherever the cooperative movement was successful and generated large institutions, it tended to become assimiliated to capitalist society. When the cooperative institutions became big they had to hire full-time managers who then did not feel part of the radical movement and began to administer the cooperatives as if they were capitalist institutions. And the attempt to survive and do well in a capitalist economy made them engage in competitive practices and become indistinguishable from privately owned companies.

Still, cooperatism remains a spiritual force in society. In our own day, many new cooperative ventures spring up in society, carried by a philosophy critical of capitalism and giving expression to a more social understanding of human life.[21] The same spirit finds expression in many other economic experiments that introduce democracy at the workplace. In some countries workers are able to become shareholders of their industries and hence share in the profit, which by itself does not yet mean that they are able to influence policy-making and assure that capital serve labor. In other countries, workers have been given a place on the boards that manage the industries. While in some cases these are token gestures offered to workers where ownership surrenders no power whatever, in others such participation has some influence on policy and the use of capital. In some capitalist countries there are attempts to involve management, labor and government in a joint planning of an industrial policy. We find similar experiments in countries that call themselves socialist. Yugoslavia in particular is famous for introducing cooperative ownership and joint control in their industries. Pope John Paul II praises all these experiments as pointing in the direction in which society must move.

The struggle for democracy at the workplace, recommended by the encyclical, can be understood in a radical and a moderate way. Some Catholics will think of themselves as following Church teaching when they wrestle for modest improvements of the present system in the direction of greater co-responsibility, while others will think that the call to economic democracy demands a repudiation of capitalism and a struggle for a radical reconstruction of society.

Soviet bloc communism has a highly centralized economic system and provides for no co-responsibility of workers. Even the non-communist, socialist parties of Western Europe ask for the public ownership of the industries and the financial institutions with little attention given to democracy at the workplace. Still, the original socialist aspirations of Marx himself included the co-responsibility of workers. The Polish workers of Solidarity demanding the right of co-determination rightfully refer to Marx against the Leninist system that oppresses them. Already the young Marx developed a theory of alienation that had application to workers in the factory.[22] He argued that whenever people are deprived of co-responsibility for the institutions to which they belong, they are deprived of part of their humanity and suffer serious alienation. This radical democratic principle was applied by Marx to all institutions, to the state in particular, but also to the economic institutions of production and exchange. Here the right to co-determination has an even stronger basis. According to Marx, workers are the owners of the goods they produce.[23] The capital which is derived from their labor belongs to them, not to the owners of the machines. From this joint ownership of the goods produced flows the right of workers to conduct their industries and determine the use of capital. While neither Marx nor Pope John Paul II uses the term "the democratization of industry," both of them agree that it is only the cooperative responsibility of workers for their industries that can overcome the workers' alienation.

Since the papal teaching on labor is similar to Marx's own theory, it is important to clarify the difference between the two. We have already noted that while for Marx labor meant principally industrial labor, the encyclical offers a much wider concept of labor, one that includes all work connected with production, from the floor cleaners to management, plus the building of the society that sustains production. In the perspective of the encyclical, modern society is a laboring society.

The most famous principle of Marxist economics is that the goods produced belong to the workers who made them, not to the owners of the industrial machinery. The capital produced by labor belongs to labor. In this perspective, wage labor appears as a form of slavery. Wage laborers, even when well paid, are robbed of the ownership of what they have produced and of the co-responsibility for the use of their product. In capitalism, Marx noted, the products of the industry belong to the owner of the machinery, who pays wages to the workers—enough to feed them and assure that they remain strong workers. The amount of capital that remains to the owner after the wages have been paid, "the surplus value of labor" in Marxist terminology, is then spent by the owner to expand his industries, or reinvested in other enterprises, or used simply for his private purposes. According to Marxist theory, this is theft. The "surplus value" of labor actually belongs to the workers who have produced it; it is up to them to decide how this capital should be used, whether it should serve the expansion of the industry, serve the needs of the workers, or serve the common good of society. According to a messianic note of classical Marxism, socialism will produce conditions under which workers shall be freed from drudgery, it shall no longer be necessary to work so hard, when surplus value shall no longer be needed, when people shall produce only what society needs and not more, and when the main energy of workers shall flow into cultural creativity and the joyful life.

What is Pope John Paul II's view of the relationship of labor and ownership? We recall that the Pope comes from a country within the Soviet bloc where the industries are not privately owned, not owned by the workers, but owned by the public, which here means the state; the use of capital in these countries is determined by the government without the participation of the workers. The workers, moreover, are paid wages as they are in capitalism. But since in principle they have no right to form independent unions, they have no power at their disposal to demand higher wages or influence the conditions of labor. In a sense, Marx's theory of labor is as critical of communism as it is of capitalism.

Pope John Paul II argues persuasively that it is a mistake to focus the discussion of the relationship of capital and labor on the ownership question. What is crucial is the *use* of capital. Many forms of ownership may be legitimate, but all of them, whether private or public, are conditional. "The only legitimate title to the possession (of the means of production), whether this be in the form of private ownership or in the form of collective ownership, is that they should serve labor" (n.14). We have here a dynamic understanding of ownership, a non-identity definition in a capitalist and communist context, which brings out the distance between what is and what ought to be and thus serves as a guide to action. One marvels again at the encyclical's fidelity to a distinct epistemological approach.

The encyclical's reflection on labor and ownership is original and deserves attention (n.14). On the one hand we are told that the laborer works for himself. Work is his own creative project despite the alienating circumstances; work is his entry into a livelihood for him and his family. This subjective dimension of work must be given priority. A society cannot be called just until the workers become in some sense the owners of the workbench at which they labor, even if this should be the giant workbench of modern industry. At the same time, in doing his work the laborer does not rely on his powers alone. Through working, the encyclical says, the worker enters upon two inheritances: the natural resources given by God to the whole human family, and the instruments of work which have been produced by the labor of men and women over generations (n.14). Personal work is therefore eminently social. *Because of this relationship to the work of others, it is wrong to say with Marx that the goods produced belong to the workers who made them and to no one else.* What follows from these considerations, rather, is that labor is both eminently personal and eminently social, that there is no easy formula in respect to ownership that corresponds to these differing aspects, and that therefore several schemes of ownership may be quite legitimate, including the private ownership of the means of production, as long as—and this is the crucial condition—the use of this capital actually serves labor, that is, ultimately, the laboring society.

What does this radical principle mean in practice? Workers dedicated to justice in countries where industries are owned by the government need not invert the economic system; all they must do is to struggle for the participation of workers in determining the conditions of labor and the use of capital. And in countries where the means of production are largely in private hands, workers committed to justice need not invert the economic system, even if it be necessary to socialize certain industries, as long as they struggle for participation in directing the use of capital and (as we shall see later) for political conditions that permit the over-all planning of the industries.

The encyclical repeatedly alludes to the possible necessity of nationalizing certain industries, even though it recognizes that in and by itself this offers no guarantee whatever that workers will be able to exercise their responsibility at the workplace and co-determine economic policy. Nationalized industries can be as much opposed to the subject character of the workers as privately owned industries. The encyclical speaks of "socializing" property only in the special case when collective ownership permits the co-determination of workers. Not all nationalization is socialization. "We can speak of socializing only when the subject character of society is ensured, that is to say, when on the basis of his work each person is fully entitled to consider himself a part owner of the great workbench at which he is working with everyone else" (n.14). Then follows a principle applicable to capitalist and communist society: "A way toward that goal can be found by associating labor with the ownership of capital" (n.14).

When the encyclical speaks of the subject character of society and the workers' co-ownership of the giant workbench, it presents the vision that must inspire the social struggle. Yet at this time, for the majority of people, it is wages that distribute the capital produced by society. Through wages people have access to the goods and services they need; through wages they share in the riches produced by labor. True, as long as workers are excluded from co-determination, there is an element of alienation in wage labor. Still, what must be demanded immediately are just wages (n.14).

The demand for just wages is a traditional Catholic principle. In Western societies this principle seemed out of date because in capitalism wages are determined on the labor market according to the law of demand and supply; and even when this rigid capitalism was transformed through the labor movement and progressive government legislation into what the encyclical calls "neo-capitalism," wages were determined by several factors, including collective bargaining, without any reference to justice. The only useful function of the Catholic demand for a just wage was that it legitimated the struggle of workers for higher wages and pensions as a moral enterprise. In the Eastern communist countries, however, there is no labor market. Prices and wages are determined by the appropriate government bureau. In this context the demand for just wages is highly significant. Workers must be remunerated for their work so that they and their families can live adequately in modest comfort. Following its wide definition of work, the encyclical insists that people who do not work in the industries but contribute to the building up of society deserve remuneration by this society. This includes mothers who choose to stay at home to look after their children. The encyclical argues that because of the present state of capitalism and communism, the key issue of social ethics is the remuneration for labor. Remuneration here refers to wages, but it also includes other aids— health plans, accident insurance, old age pensions, etc. (n.19).

In this context of the struggle for justice, the encyclical discusses the nature and role of labor unions. "The experience of history teaches that organizations of this type are an indispensable element of social life, especially in modern industrialized societies" (n.20). This does not mean, the encyclical adds, that only industrial workers have the right to unionize. This right is shared by all workers in the widest sense: agricultural, white-collar, scientific and professional. While the encyclical regards the workers' struggle for justice as indispensable, in fact as the dynamic principle of contemporary history, it distinguishes this struggle from "the class struggle" in the Marxist sense. The unions are not simply reflections of the class struggle defined by the objective conditions of economic production; they do not follow a necessary law operative in history; they do not engage in a war against the ruling class or against the bosses whom they seek to conquer. Instead, the "class struggle" in the sense of the encyclical is grounded in the free choice of workers to respond to the objective conditions of oppression with solidarity and common struggle. While this struggle for justice is the "normal endeavor" (n.20) operative in society, it is not the result of intrinsic necessity. Even when in many cases the struggle of unions takes on "the character of opposition toward others" (n.20), in actual fact it aims first and foremost at social justice, and turns against others only to the extent that these others, the rulers or the bosses, obstruct the way toward greater justice. Moreover, since the struggle for justice aims at establishing the priority of labor over capital, labor unions promote the unity and the well-being of the whole people. Union demands are not simply expressions of their own collective self-interest, of a kind of "class egoism" as the encyclical calls it (n.20); they are expressions of the struggle to make capital serve labor, which means serve the laborers of the union (collective self-interest), serve the advancement of the industry, and finally serve the entire laboring community. In this sense "union activity enters the field of politics" (n.20). The workers' struggle as defined by the encyclical reaches out toward the transformation of society. "Union demands can and should also aim at correcting—with a view to the common good of the whole society—everything defective in the system of ownership of the means of production or in the way these are managed" (n.20). The workers' struggle through union activity has a critical political function both in the capitalist societies of the West and in the communist societies of the East.

Since the workers' struggle as understood by the encyclical is based on freedom and solidarity and aims at the reconstruction of society in justice, it is essentially a moral endeavor. It is not the work of historical necessity. The encyclical has "dereified" the Marxist concept and brought out the freedom and responsibility operative in the labor movement. Pope John Paul II shows that union activity must be guided by a set of moral norms. We have already mentioned some of them: union activity serves justice, demands justice not only for itself but for all workers and for society as a whole, aims at transforming the economic system or its management, and ultimately promotes the unity of society. While union activity reaches into politics, the encyclical says that a union should not "play politics." Unions do not have the character of political parties struggling for power. "They should not be subjected to the decision of political parties or have too close links with them" (n.20). For some reason or other, this sentence has often been cited in the American press. It plays an altogether minor part in the encyclical's rich and daring teaching on labor unions. The sentence does suggest that the Pope addresses himself here to the Polish labor union Solidarity.

Pope John Paul II also recommends that unions foster labor schools for their members. In this context, he praises workers' or people's universities that offer training programs to workers in matters dealing with the labor movement but also in wider cultural education.

Catholic social teaching has regarded the strike as a legitimate measure in the labor struggle, under the appropriate conditions and within just limits. The encyclical confirms this: "In this connection workers should be assured of the right to strike, without being subjected to personal penal sanctions for taking part in the strike. While admitting that it is a legitimate means, we must at the same time emphasize that a strike remains, in a sense, an extreme means. It must not be abused; it must not be abused, especially, for 'political' purposes" (n.20). Again, one has the feeling that the Pope was speaking directly to Solidarity.

The encyclical does not deal directly with the issue of labor unions and strikes in the capitalist societies. It provides, as we have seen, several useful principles, but does not examine the complex reality of the labor movement nor counsel Catholic workers how to involve themselves in it. The workers' struggles in capitalist countries are inspired by differing social philosophies, even if it is not always easy to discern these from the actual union strategies. Some unions simply struggle for a fairer deal for their members. In a minimal way, this falls within the norms of justice outlined in the encyclical. Yet unions may be so affected by the capitalist approach that they strive for the most they can get; they argue that this is in fact the spirit of the market system. Sometimes labor unions find themselves overwhelmed by power struggles which affect their policies in an adverse manner. Usually union struggles are associated with a particu-

lar vision of society. The labor struggle is here part of a wider social
project. Some workers opt for the type of society the encyclical calls
"neo-capitalist," i.e., for a form of capitalism that, while protecting
the interests of capitalists, allows workers a certain share in the
wealth of society and provides welfare for the poor and unemployed,
even if it opposes the co-determination and co-ownership of workers.
In the past, workers sometimes opted for communism; they desired a
socialist society and believed that they could trust the leadership of
the Soviet Union. The strategies of unions in control of communists
had to be understood in terms of the over-all planning of Soviet-guid-
ed international communism. A great many workers were, and still
are, inspired by a home-grown socialist vision of society in accordance with the aspirations of their own nation. They struggle for the
rights of their members as part of a larger socialist project. They are
deeply concerned about all workers, not just those of their own
union, they are committed to the unemployed and the poor in their
own country, they promote the cause of labor and of the poor in other parts of the world, and they seek the support not only of their
class but of the people as a whole. They strive for a social order in
which capital is made to serve labor, which includes serving the entire laboring society. This latter approach seems to me the way in
which the encyclical envisages the labor struggle.

Sometimes workers are inspired by resentment derived from
prolonged oppression and decide to join sectarian political movements that try to undermine the operation of the existing society, according to the principle "the worse, the better." They hope that a
breakdown of the present system will lead to the creation of a more
humane society. Such an approach is wholly at odds with the encyclical.

While the encyclical provides inspiration for Catholic workers
and some guidance, it does not deal with the concrete problems that
pose themselves in our societies. Pope John Paul, we noted, demanded that the workers' struggle also aim at the promotion of the industries in which they labor. This poses difficult questions when these
industries are involved in the production of arms, in particular nuclear weapons, or when industries that have become outmoded and re-
fuse to change demand government subsidies to survive. What the
encyclical affirms without any reservation is the unionization of la-

bor. Within the labor movement it favors those forces that express themselves in terms of justice, envisage the transformation of society, and promote the unity of the people.

The encyclical's demand for the workers' co-determination is a principle of decentralization. The papal document puts great stress on decentralization because the communist economies of the East and even the economic policies of the socialist parties in the West are centralist. They envisage the government alone as responsible for planning the economy. Still, after the stress on the workers' co-determination the encyclical turns to the complementary demand for central planning, without which capital cannot be made to serve labor. There is no way of getting around this. In a society where the industries are interrelated and depend in their operation on many functions exercised by society, such as communication, transportation, schools and housing, to mention only the most obvious, production and distribution cannot be left to the free interplay of the market, which always favors the rich and powerful; nor can it be left to the economic giants, the transnationals, which plan the economy in view of maximizing their own profit. Because of the nature of industrialized society economic planning has become necessary (n.18). We need a rational plan for the economy, to be worked out through collaboration of the various sectors of society, which the government adopts and puts into practice. Because of maldistribution of raw materials and wealth in the world, the Pope envisages that the planning of the economy through national governments will eventually have to involve international consultation so that the poorer nations will not be excluded from the earth's resources (n.18). The tension between the two principles, the principle of de-centralization (the democratization of the industries) and the principle of centralization (the planned economy), constitutes a dynamic process in society that protects the well-being of all and the relative freedom of persons and groups of persons.

The workers' struggle for the priority of labor over capital calls for two distinct strategies: the union movement to achieve workers' participation in the industries and the political movement to obtain the kind of government that will involve society in the planning of the economy. Let it be said that the demand for a planned economy is not new for Pope John Paul II. Already in his first encyclical, he maintained that the economic problems of present day society are such that reliance on the free interplay of various industries is no longer feasible; what is needed is "an authentically human plan."[24] Without such a plan society will become increasingly unjust; ever larger sections of the population will be pushed into unemployment, poverty, and social misery.

To clarify the need for a planned economy in our day, *Laborem exercens* offers a detailed analysis of the problem of unemployment. It introduces a useful distinction between the "direct" and the "indirect" employer (n.17). The direct employer is the employer in the usual sense; it is the person or group of persons that makes a contract with the worker in regard to the work to be done and the remuneration to be received. In contemporary society, however, there are many societal factors that influence the contract between the worker and the direct employer; these factors are called "indirect employer." Such factors include, for example, government legislation regarding the conditions of employment, the training of workers available at schools or other institutions, systems of transport that enable workers to get to the office or factory, and the availability of houses sufficiently close to the place of work. Because of the complexity of modern industrial society and the interconnectedness of all its functions, the indirect employer is society itself. Questions of employment and unemployment touch the whole of society. And the whole of society is responsible for them.

Two important consequences follow from the distinction between the direct and indirect employer. The first is that the problem of unemployment can only be solved if we recognize the reality of the indirect employer. It is totally unrealistic to expect that the present crisis of unemployment can be overcome by the initiatives of the direct employers, that is to say, through the expansion of existing industries or the creation of new ones by private corporations. Why? Because this aim is not in keeping with their purpose to advance themselves. To overcome unemployment the indirect employer, that is, society as a whole, must be involved. This is the argument for a planned economy. What is necessary is government action that protects workers on their job, that creates training programs preparing workers for the work needed in society, that fosters an industrial policy which plans production in view of the available resources and the presence of a market, possibly with international consultation, and that provides housing, transportation, and training to promote these industrial goals. The papal encyclical defends a viewpoint diametrically opposed to the policy of the Reagan administration. It is, however, in accord with government policy of the social-democratic or socialist parties of Western Europe, which regard government as responsible for the full employment of workers. In this political context, it is possible and necessary to speak of the right to work. In fact, the Pope affirms the right to work as belonging to the human rights (n.16). The encyclical deals with a whole set of rights of labor (n.16), including rights of immigrants and the disabled (nn.22–23).

The other consequence following from the distinction between direct and indirect employer is an important corrective for the communist societies of the Soviet bloc. Here society must be reminded that the emphasis on the indirect employer, and hence on the responsibility of government for the employment of workers, must not overlook the direct employer. The direct employer is not simply an agent of society; it is important to defend the freedom of workers to deal directly with the industries that hire them, to search for the kind of work that is suitable to their talents and appealing to their mind, and to leave their job after a certain period defined by the contract. The encyclical, here as always, while stressing the unity of society, also defends freedom and flexibility at the local level.

Laborem exercens envisages a central planning that involves the participation of many institutions. Government itself is not the planning agency. Pluralism must be institutionalized even in the economic infrastructure. The encyclical speaks of "a wide range of intermediate bodies" with economic purposes, enjoying "real autonomy with regard to the public powers" and pursuing their aim "in honest collaboration with each other and in subordination to the demands of the common good" (n.14).

The political struggle for a planned economy must therefore not be separated from the social struggle for democracy at the workplace. In the past, one of the arguments offered by Catholic social teaching against socialism was precisely that a government capable of controlling the economy had too much power and endangered the survival of local units which protected human freedom. Over the last decade, papal teaching has come to recognize that in Western society the danger of domination comes in the first instance from the large transnational corporations, not from the state, and for this reason it has been willing to advocate that government exercise a greater role in the economy. The traditional principle of subsidiarity, which was designed to protect the small units capable of looking after their needs from interference by a higher power, was complemented by the principle of socialization, enunciated especially by Pope John XXIII, which stated that whenever smaller units are unable to provide for their members, then higher levels of authority must promote cooperation so that people will be protected.[25] Small is beautiful, but big whenever necessary. In industrial society, big is unavoidable. The creative tension between the principles of subsidiarity and socialization is replayed in the present encyclical in the double demand for democracy at the workplace and for the planning of the economy.

Reading *Laborem exercens* it is impossible not to think of Yugoslavia, the Eastern European country that made itself independent from Russian communism in 1948 and developed its own style of socialism. What characterizes Yugoslav society is the tension between two complementary principles: there is the over-all planning of the economy by the government and some government ownership, especially of the larger industries, and there are the small units of production and services, co-owned by the workers who collectively promote the advancement of their own industries. There is room in Yugoslavia for private ownership of productive machinery. It is possible to own and profit from small units of production if the number of employees is below five. Once an enterprise has five employees law demands that it be owned by the workers and that they be responsible for its policy. The tension between the government responsible for planning the over-all economy and the many cooperatively operated industries is meant to protect freedom and creativity in the country. What is unfortunate in Yugoslavia is that the profound divisions of the country along ethnic and religious lines has tempted the government to adopt an official social philosophy, a form of Marxism, in the hope that a secular national ideology will promote unity and overcome the various religious identifications associated with the ethnic groups or peoples within the country. This secular ideology is hostile to religion and hence prevents ordinary people attached to their faith from freely participating in the building up of their country.[26] However imperfect the Yugoslav economic system may be, it does bear a certain resemblance to the socialism outlined in *Laborem exercens.*

Laborem exercens also reminds the reader of the present economic order in Nicaragua. Here the revolutionary democratic government undertakes the over-all planning of the economy while leaving room for privately and collectively owned enterprises.[27] The government thinks that through its legislative power and the nationalization of certain key institutions it can guide the economy of the country in a manner that encourages the enterprise of productive and commercial companies. Since the small country is exposed to strong external pressures, especially by those who think that its successful revolutionary experiment should not be allowed to stand, no one knows how long the present order will last.

But what does the teaching of the encyclical mean in capitalist countries such as the United States and Canada? The twofold struggle for the democratization of the industries and the over-all planning of the economy is certainly at odds with the capitalist heritage and the dominant social philosophy. Still, even in Western society we find movements that correspond to the double direction set forth in *Laborem exercens.* There are movements that seek to introduce cooperative principles in various economic institutions, and there are political movements that favor a government ready to introduce economic and industrial policies to protect the well-being of the people. We shall return to this topic further on.

Technology as Ally

The encyclical *Laborem exercens,* as a theological document, recognizes the world as a place of sin. The present crisis in the societies of East and West is due to failures that are structural as well as moral. This has always been the emphasis of papal social teaching. Economic crises, the causes of so much suffering, have two dimensions, a structural and a moral one, both of which deserve careful analysis. Until now we have examined the structural cause of oppression, namely the economic systems that violate the priority of labor over capital. What we need is a struggle to change the present economic systems in East and West. But where does the encyclical locate the moral failure? Contemporary ecclesiastical documents have taken up the notion of "social sin." The encyclical offers the theory that a great moral wrong was committed by the early capitalists who decided to organize their capital against the workers who had produced it (n.11). This disruption of the moral order, we are told, led to a false economic theory, which in turn made the opposition between capital and labor universal in modern society. This state of affairs, the encyclical tells us, must eventually be changed through the workers' struggle for justice. The moral failure or sin in this case lies in the powerful who oppose justice in society. The workers, we are told, are not struggling *against* a group of people, they are fighting *for* justice, and only to the extent that those who control capital resist the way of justice does the workers' movement become a struggle against the powerful, in other words a class struggle. Since the encyclical envisages the workers' struggle as a moral endeavor, ultimately aimed at reconciliation and cooperation in justice, narrowly selfish aims and irrational demands of workers are also sins that may contribute to the conditions of oppression.

Social sin also resides in the creation of the rigid ideologies, economic liberalism and determinist Marxism, which have presented reified images of the real conflicts in society and prevented people from understanding their historical situation and the possibilities of overcoming the existing injustice. These ideologies, we are told, have guided the workers' movements into errors and made them the sources of oppression, and they have led the capitalist class and its allies to devise social policies that have caused untold harm (n.11). According to the encyclical, the structural contradictions of economic and political systems are never simply the result of necessity based on economic laws; they are humanly inspired contradictions and hence have the character of sin.

In a previous document, Pope John Paul II offered another theory to account for the contradictions of society. It is useful to recall it at this point.[28] In his first encyclical the Pope argued that many institutions, including economic ones, were established by people to meet the needs of their times. As the historical conditions changed many people discovered that these institutions no longer served them, but by that time the institutions had acquired a weight and momentum of their own, they operated out of a logic built into them at the start, and people found that it was very difficult if not impossible to change them. The structures man created for his benefit became, after an historical development, a source of oppression. Such a dialectical view of societal contradictions would allow the theologian to speak of "social sin" without having to claim that there was personal sin in the original setting up of the institution. "Social sin" would then lie in the oppressive conditions produced by the institution at a later time, and in people's unwillingness to recognize this condition and to struggle against it, or even in some people's opposition to change.

For *Laborem exercens,* as for contemporary liberation theology, the root cause of evil in society is located in its injustices, that is to say, in its oppressive conditions. There are social thinkers and theologians who offer an alternative sociology of evil. They argue that the contemporary cause of universal dehumanization is not social injustice but the technological nature of modern society. The increasing influence of technology, accompanied by the bureaucratization of society, gradually depersonalizes human existence and alienates man from his own freedom. All qualities are transformed into quantities; all social processes become subject to technical control; every aspect of social life, including education, art, religion and entertainment, becomes bureaucratized and programmed; even the realm of the personal and intimate is progressively invaded by a technological imagination of usefulness and control. What we experience in modern industrial society is the death of human creativity.

This sociology of alienation has its roots in German social thought, especially in the writings of Ferdinand Toennies and Max Weber.[29] It was also reflected in existentialist philosophy where society was understood as an ever present pressure of depersonalization, the "man" in the language of Heidegger, against which the person seeking authenticity had to affirm himself. This sociology of alienation has been elaborated by contemporary social scientists in North America. Peter Berger, in particular, has tried to show that industrial society creates "mega-structures," big industry, big business, big government, big unions, and that as a result all people, to whatever social level they may belong, experience depersonalization and powerlessness.[30] Berger argues that socialists misread the malaise of modernity; they believe that oppression or injustice is the principal cause of modern unhappiness while in actual fact it is the mega-structures of technocracy, inevitably associated with industrial growth, that cause unhappiness and create a sense of homelessness among people. Dehumanization, therefore, threatens not only the poor, the workers, and the lower sector of society; it also threatens the well-to-do and the powerful. Those who want to struggle for the humanization of life in modern society should not wrestle against class divisions and social inequalities; instead they should create small communities, "mediating structures," which allow people caught in mega-structures during their hours of work to belong to small social frameworks where life is still mediated in an interpersonal manner. The malaise of modernity is here to stay; what we must do therefore is to create mediating structures in the interstices of the great society, such as neighborhoods, housing colonies, ethnic associations, and religious groupings, in which to protect our personhood from becoming more and more dehumanized.

This sociology of alienation has had a considerable influence on Christian theology. The best known author is here the French Protestant theologian Jacques Ellul, widely translated into English, who sees the technological society of our day as the source of all dehumanization.[31] He tries to show that the technological framework in which we live destroys everything that is genuinely human—human relations, beauty, social ideals, the exchange of ideas, and the public utterance of truth. Man has become part of the mega-machine. Peter Berger, writing as a Christian thinker, regrets that the churches have permitted themselves to be influenced by persons sympathetic to socialism, and that they have come to regard social injustice as the principal enemy of human well-being and in some parts of the world even support people's liberation movements. Peter Berger argues that instead the churches should adopt as pastoral policy the transformation of parishes into "mediating structures," that is to say, into communities built into the interstices of industrial society where the loyalty to the higher reality of the transcendent God helps people to constitute true fellowship among themselves and through this save their own humanity.

The encyclical *Laborem exercens* follows the sociology of alienation taken from the socialist intellectual tradition. The key concept for understanding the construction of society and the crises of this society is labor. The dehumanizing trends in society must be analyzed around the structures of human labor. In contemporary society, the source of oppression is the economic system that violates the priority of labor over capital. And the great task that faces humanity is the struggle of the oppressed, joined in solidarity by those who love justice, to reconstruct the economic system so that capital may come to serve labor.

The approach of the encyclical to technology is appropriately different from the negativism of the authors mentioned above (n.5). As the encyclical rejects the reified view of society and the corresponding ideology of determinist Marxism, so it also rejects the reified perception of technology and any theory defining its inevitable and necessary consequences. Pope John Paul II repudiates any form of determinism. Technology is not a single reality; it is made up of many kinds, of many trends, of many instances, and in each case we must examine whether its impact is helpful or harmful to human beings.

Pope John Paul II declares, "Technology is undoubtedly man's ally" (n.5). This is the view of man the laborer. Technology facilitates work: it perfects, accelerates and augments it. It leads to an increase in the quantity produced and in many instances improves their quality. The encyclical acknowledges destructive effects of technology in circumscribed terms. "In some instances technology can cease to be man's ally and becomes almost his enemy" (n.5). This sentence sets the encyclical apart from the universal lament over technology that pervades a good deal of sociological, existential and theological writing. Technology becomes enemy, the encyclical says, when the mechanization of work supplants the worker, taking away all personal satisfaction and the incentive to creativity and responsibility. Technology becomes enemy when it substitutes itself for tasks assigned to workers and creates unemployment. It becomes enemy when through exalting the machine man is reduced to the status of a slave. There is no hint in the encyclical that technology has an overall alienating effect in modern society. There is no sense in which technology has become the great metaphor of society transforming it into a machine and reducing people to mechanical parts of the giant apparatus. There is here no existentialist gloom accusing technology of undermining personal human relations, damaging the appreciation of art and culture, wounding fatally man's openness to religion and initiating him into the iron cage, the computerized prison house.

Pope John Paul II looks upon technology from the viewpoint of industrial and agricultural labor. Technology delivers people from drudgery, it becomes for them a reliable tool, it summons forth new skills in them, it makes more demands on their mind and less on their muscles. Technology only becomes enemy when it routinizes work excessively and creates boredom or when it replaces workers and leads to unemployment. Technology becomes hostile to workers when management, for the sake of greater efficiency, power and profit, decides to use technology against the workers, against their good. Technology as such has very limited intrinsic power. Man ever

remains the subject of technology (n.5); when it has deadly consequences it is because the people who control it have made deadly decisions.

The same kind of clarity characterizes the brief references of the
encyclical to the ecological crisis of our times. Pope John Paul II recognizes "the growing realization that the heritage of nature is limited
and that it is being intolerably polluted" (n.1), but he sees this problem as part of the moral challenge that accompanies the use and development of technology. The Pope continues to speak of technology
in an affirmative way. Since man remains always subject, and since
the technological equipment remains always instrument, people and
human well-being are the appropriate measure of technology. While
the encyclical makes several references to "the threat of nuclear war
and the prospect of the terrible permanent self-destruction that
emerges from it" (n.2), it does not suggest that the development of
nuclear technology itself exceeds man's vocation to utilize nature
and that for this reason it should be avoided by society. At other
times Pope John Paul has taken a very strong stand against the continued increase of nuclear armament, a stand in which many bishops
all over the world have recently supported him,[32] but in this encyclical his main point is that man is responsible for the production and
use of technology and that the threats to human peace and the survival of humanity can only be overcome when the agencies that control capital can be forced to make this capital serve labor. No
lamenting over the destructive use of technology nor even over the
development of nuclear weapons will do any good in the long run until the workers can participate in decision-making and until governments, in international consultation, plan the production of foods
and goods for the well-being of the entire working humanity. For the
encyclical the ecological crisis can be overcome through the introduction of a socialist economy. We must struggle for political and
economic systems in which the decisions regarding the development
and use of technology are made in the interest of labor.

That the encyclical says so little about the threat of nuclear war
seems strange, especially since Pope John Paul II has such strong
views regarding the matter. Because the encyclical deals with labor,
the Pope wants to relate the threat of war to labor. Only a few hints

are made. Pius XI in *Quadragesimo Anno* (1931), written during the great depression, argued that monopoly capitalism led to economic dictatorship, to a new form of imperialism and hence to new forms of conflicts between nations.[33] War would be the ultimate result. The causes of war are here connected with economics. Pope John Paul II only makes a few remarks on this topic. His encyclical attributes the conflict between nations and empires to economic inequalities and more especially to the erroneous ideologies that the two sides of the conflict have created which blind them in regard to the historical reality and steer them into conflicts and the quest for domination (nn.3–4).

Laborem exercens is a hopeful document. It is free of the typically Western gloom. In this context it is interesting to look at the manner in which the encyclical cites the Book of Genesis and the divine command given to man "to subdue the earth" and to exercise "dominion over the earth." These biblical texts are crucial for Pope John Paul II. It is with their help that the encyclical develops the concept of man as worker. The papal document never refers to the controversy among Western theologians as to whether the biblical teaching of "subduing" the earth and of man's "dominion" over the earth has been a contributing factor to the present ecological crisis. Why did Western society dominate nature so ruthlessly? Why did we exploit it beyond measure? Why did we look upon nature as a quarry to be exploited without regard for its integrity? Some writers have suggested that an important cultural cause of the ecological crisis is the biblical teaching that man's task is to conquer nature.[34] Nature here is seen simply as an instrument for human well-being. This argument, in my opinion, is not convincing. The biblical command to subdue the earth and to exercise dominion over it was given to an agricultural people. It was a call to become cultivators of the earth and stewards of the riches stored up in nature. Agricultural people know that nature must not be violated, for if you subjugate nature, you make it barren and destroy it. It was only with the emergence of industrialization in the hands of the entrepreneurs that man's relationship to nature underwent a change. Now the driving force behind man's dominion over nature was the maximization of power and profit. Not biblical teaching but a profit-oriented economy is responsible for the devastation of nature. Still, Western theologians have begun to use the quotation from Genesis with care. They always indicate that the command "to subdue" the earth was a call to stewardship. The encyclical is free of this Western anguish. It repeatedly refers to the text from Genesis without distinguishing between an acceptable and an unacceptable "dominion" over the earth.

Man's Making of Man

Let us continue to explore the encyclical's fidelity to its focus on labor. It is through labor that people create their world, and it is through the same labor that in a certain sense they also create themselves, both as the subject laboring and hence entering into self-actualization, and as people socialized by the objective conditions produced by their labor. The encyclical brings the family and national identity into this perspective. While "family" and "peoplehood" constitute values distinct from labor, they are nonetheless intimately connected with labor as the primary reality (n.10).

We are told that labor lays the foundation for the family. Labor produces the material conditions in which families can live and thrive. At the same time, family life reflects back on the laboring society because in the family children are socialized and made ready to labor. The family is the first school of labor (n.10). The encyclical only makes a brief reference to this interconnection, yet in doing so it opens a new perspective on the family which Catholic social teaching has not explored until now. In the first place, if labor lays the foundation for the family, then unemployment, underpaid work, and damaging and humiliating conditions of labor must be seen as factors affecting family life. Conversely, if the family is the novitiate of labor for society then the family is not free of its own conditions of alienation. For if an economic system refuses to allow workers to participate in the decision-making process affecting their work, then this organization of labor is likely to be mirrored in the family, the primary school of labor. This principle has profound implications for the role of women in society. On the other hand, if the family introduces children to work in the context of cooperation and co-determination, then their socialization, at odds with the prevailing system, has its own political weight and consequences. While these matters are not discussed in the encyclical, the link that this document establishes between the family and the primacy of labor opens the door to such reflections. Until now Catholic social thought has shied away from examining the conditions of alienation within the family and the socio-political impact of child-raising.

The encyclical also looks upon peoplehood in relation to labor. Again we only have a few important hints. The nation, "the great society to which man belongs on the basis of particular cultural and historical links" (n.10), is the principal educator of people, even though this education is indirect since it is for the most part directly exercised by the family. Nationhood is educator as matrix of language, as defining a style of human interaction and generating social ideals, and as such it affects labor. Conversely, the national society is itself "the great historical and social incarnation of all generations" (n.10). For the child born into it, the nation is a given in which he or she is being socialized. Yet historically speaking, the nation is not a given; it has been produced by human labor and human engagement. The nation then is something that people have made themselves, and yet something that is now part of them. We notice the dialectical reasoning. And because man "combines his deepest human identity with membership in a nation" (n.10), he understands his labor to be of service to the well-being of his own people—and only after that, following a more universal concern, to be of service to all people living on earth.

The encyclical does not attempt to deal with the difficult question of how to define what a nation or what peoplehood is. This question is of crucial importance today to peoples struggling to define their historical existence. The merit of the few remarks the encyclical makes on the subject is that it relates peoplehood to labor and thereby opens the door to reflections that are new in Catholic social teaching. Since labor is at one and the same time the expression of man's creativity and the bearer of human alienation, the nation itself, and nationalism, is not without its own ambiguity. For the nation which is the great educator may in fact be the embodiment of unjust social structures and protect the opposition of capital to labor. At the same time the nation or nationalism may generate ideals of solidarity and mutual sharing which are at odds with the existing organization of labor and hence inspire people in their struggle for justice.

It may be helpful to introduce a distinction which the encyclical does not make but which is in accordance with its spirit. We distinguish between "economic labor" and "social labor." What the encyclical calls simply labor is really economic or productive labor. Economic labor includes production, the organization of labor, the distribution of resources and goods, and the organization of society, including systems of law, communication, transportation, etc., making possible the production and distribution of goods. The anthropological basis for this labor is man's biological need for food and shelter and man's innate rational ability to create the instruments for the satisfaction of his biological needs. Economic labor, however, does not exhaust human labor. In fact, the economic organization could not work unless it were aided by another form of labor, namely "social labor." Social labor includes language, family, peoplehood, and spirituality or religion. Economic production is in need of language for communication, in need of family for the socialization of young people ready to work, in need of peoplehood for the over-all cohesiveness of the social project, and in need of spirituality or inwardness to guide workers in the exercise of their tasks. Social labor serves the material needs of the human family. While economic and social labor are essential elements of man's historical self-constitution, the encyclical gives priority to economic labor which it calls simply labor.

We notice that in its equation of labor with economic labor the encyclical follows the Marxist usage even though it has expanded the notion of labor to include all work done by society that contributes to production. Marxism on the whole tends to neglect social labor (language, family, peoplehood, spirituality). Pope John Paul II greatly emphasizes it. What is new in his social teaching—new for Catholics—is that he assigns priority to economic labor and understands social labor as serving the laboring society. Family, peoplehood, and (as we shall see) spirituality are conceived as contributing to society built up in justice.

Allow me at this point to summarize the encyclical's theory of man's self-constitution through labor.

Man is obliged to labor if he wants to live. Man must wrestle with nature; he must transform a portion of nature through labor to have food and shelter. In order to improve the conditions of survival, people must invent a division of labor, a social organization, and a system of authority. Labor creates society. Labor is helped in doing this by language, family, ethnic identity and unitive symbols—in other words, by a world of culture, whose origin and basic function may be defined by their relationship to labor, even though the values implicit in them have also meaning in themselves, apart from labor. Because these human endeavors (we have called them "social labor" above) are prompted by labor and in turn serve labor, it is possible to say that man creates his world, his history and therefore in a sense also himself. Man can be said to constitute himself by labor because he is subject and because he actualizes himself above all through labor. Through laboring man becomes more truly human. Through laboring man becomes capable of exercising responsibility for his history. Conversely, man can be said to constitute himself because through his labor he creates the world which then socializes him, affects his consciousness, and shapes his powers and interests. Man the subject is therefore also in some sense object. It is possible to speak of man's making of man.

While it is possible to speak of man's self-constitution through labor, something is given about the human being. First, given is nature or the portion of nature that man needs to create the conditions of his survival. The Christian sees here the hand of the Creator. Second, given is man's essential endowment as laboring subject. Man differs from animals through his rational ability to produce the instruments necessary for satisfying his material needs. Man alone labors. The Christian regards this essential endowment as God's work. But the twofold givenness mentioned here, which Christians acknowledge as God's creation, does not prevent us from speaking of man's self-constitution through labor. While man is subject from the beginning, he becomes subject of his world only through labor. In this context it is possible, even from a Christian point of view, to speak of man's making of man.

Does this understanding of man as worker overlook the spiritual? Does it neglect the sphere of values? Does it belittle man's freedom to rise above the exigencies of the material order and encounter God in prayer? The stress on the spiritual, on moral values, and on human freedom characterize the entire encyclical (24–27). The primacy of the subject and of the subjective dimension of labor means that the most important aspect of man laboring is precisely his personal transformation as subject, both in regard to his interiority and freedom and in regard to his responsibility for his world, his future and himself. But spirit, values and freedom are not introduced into human life from outside of human laboring as if coming from a higher realm; they are not imposed upon men and women by their relationship to a higher world, as it were; they emerge from the exigencies of laboring itself. Spirit is here the spirit of laboring man.[35] Values situate themselves in the struggle for life, for community, for justice. Freedom is present in men and women laboring—the encyclical even insists that this freedom never totally disappears, even under conditions of grave alienation. Freedom inspires workers to do their work faithfully and, to the extent that they suffer oppression, to generate solidarity and jointly struggle for justice.

The primacy of the subjective, of interiority, of free personal consciousness is affirmed by the encyclical in an original manner. The principle of subjectivity is applied in the "dereifying" of liberal and more especially of Marxist categories. The class struggle itself, once "dereified," and freed from the ideological perspective, reveals itself as the struggle of the oppressed, freely joining together in solidarity and fighting for justice as the only way in which they can improve their own condition and transform society. This workers' struggle then is possible only through a surrender to solidarity (which is spiritual), only if collective self-interest is accompanied by a dedication to justice (which implies values), and only if the workers recognize that history is not subject to a fixed logic but remains open to human initiative (which affirms freedom).

Even man's turning to God and man's religious experiences do not lift him out of the sphere of work to some higher form of existence. It is precisely as worker that man reaches out for an interior life that enables him to labor under harsh conditions and struggle for justice. Precisely as worker man recognizes the need for cooperation, mutual aid, selflessness and solidarity; and if he is a Christian he recognizes in the Gospel message the good news—the encyclical occasionally speaks here of "the gospel of work" (nn.6,26)—that God is present to the human struggle as the one who summons and enables men and women to leave selfishness behind and enter upon a cooperative existence, in which alone love and justice can be at home. Man the worker is, therefore, not only given over to action, but also to passion; he labors and struggles, yet, especially as believer, he also suffers divine grace as call and as power. Man does not exhaust himself in laboring; he is nourished from within by God's word and God's Spirit.

In a previous paragraph I have shown that in our age of global interconnectedness we are led to ask questions our ancestors did not pose. Why should we in the organization of our own society take into consideration the oppressed condition of third world countries? Why should the various levels of working people in their struggle for greater justice in their own country show concern for the dispossessed of the third world? It seems to me that there is no wholly secular reason for universal solidarity. The Marxist concept of working class solidarity does not apply here since the dispossessed in the third world are not workers, not yet workers. I have argued that it is only out of a faith in the unity of man, out of a sacred sense of solidarity, out of a religious awareness that we are all brothers and sisters, that people commit themselves to justice on a world scale. From a strictly material point of view, then, from the viewpoint of laboring men and women creating the conditions of their earthly life, people are in need of the God revealed in Jesus Christ. God makes humanity possible.

We may summarize these remarks by saying that the encyclical's stress on spirituality does not create a dualistic picture of man, the lower faculties occupied with material factors and the higher ones with the spiritual sphere. Spirituality, like family and peoplehood, is here understood as serving labor, as serving man laboring to become more fully subject of his history.

With its focus on labor and man laboring, the encyclical has developed a consistent methodological approach to human issues, including that of spirituality. Is there a name for this approach? It certainly negates the idealistic approach to human self-understanding. The idealistic approach begins with a dualistic picture of the human being, according to which people are confronted by two sets of issues, relatively independent from one another, the lower being defined by labor and the material conditions of life, and the higher by ideas and the world of the spirit. According to this idealistic approach, man is truly fortunate if he does not have to deal with laboring and the material factors, and if instead he can devote himself entirely to the spirit, to ideas, to higher things. This approach presupposes that the formation of human consciousness is independent of man's historical situation, and that consciousness wholly transcends the material conditions of life and soars to spiritual heights. A good deal of philosophy and theology operates in this perspective. When examining the deep and important issues in these fields of inquiry, thinkers tend to bracket the material circumstances under which people are in touch with ideas and experience the spirit. It is possible to write a whole treatise on philosophy and theology without ever adverting to the conflicts, the conditions of oppression and the struggle for justice going on in one's own country and in the world. Why? Because ideas are thought to be independent of time. Ideas are thought to be universal.

Over against this, the encyclical focuses on labor and understands ideas and spirituality in terms of their relationship to man laboring. Consciousness is here conceived as being created first of all by labor, both from the subjective point of view (man's self-actualization through labor) and from the objective point of view (man is socialized in a world largely of his own making). Even God is here understood as the gracious Presence in the midst of life, calling and empowering people in a sinful world to struggle for a more authentically human life and to become subjects of their history. Consciousness is here conceived not as floating above history, as enjoying a universality of its own, but as rooted in historical conditions, shaped through people's social location and the stance they adopt within it. Since this approach is contrary to the idealist stance, it should be possible to call it "materialist."

The encyclical does not use this terminology. On the contrary, the word "materialism" is used in an entirely pejorative sense. We are told that it was the practical materialism of the early capitalists that made them set up their capital against labor (n.7). This inversion of the right order gave rise to economic liberalism which regarded the human being as an economic unity, *homo oeconomicus,* defined in purely quantitative terms of needs and satisfactions and thus as a being whose behavior was economically determined and hence could be scientifically predicted. This economism was a practical materialism, not a theoretical one; it did not negate the spiritual realm, except that it excluded the spirit from any impact on man's economic behavior. Marxism, while wishing to overcome the liberal understanding of the human person, remained nonetheless in the economist framework. In Marxism, man remains an economic unit, defined this time not in micro-terms of needs and satisfactions but in macro-terms as an ensemble of social relations reflecting their economic base. *Laborem exercens* vehemently rejects this understanding of human being. Man the worker is man the subject. In liberalism and in Marxism, the practical materialist approach eventually generated a theoretical materialism which denied altogether the spirit and the reality of God. This error is denounced by the encyclical. More than that, it shows that this denial weakens man in his struggle to become the subject of his society. It is an ideology that blinds people, makes them interpret falsely their historical situation, and orients them toward actions that will ultimately be harmful.

At the same time, in rejecting practical and theoretical materialism the encyclical does not adopt an idealist viewpoint or promote a dualistic understanding of man. The encyclical never moves away from man the worker who produces the conditions for his collective existence, who creates society, who struggles to become the subject of his history. There seems to be no useful term to designate this anti-idealist, non-dualistic, labor-oriented approach. It is possible, I think, to call it "materialist" in this special sense.[36] In such a materialist approach, God may be recognized as the redemptive Presence in people's lives, summoning and empowering them, through labor, to become subjects of their history, both collectively and as individuals. Eternal life here is not a realm that competes with earthly life for loyalty; it is rather the unfolding of the subject character of human life beyond death.

For Christian preaching and Christian theology it is of the utmost importance to distinguish between an idealist and a materialist interpretation of the Christian message. Does the Gospel address itself to spiritual man and must we therefore bracket the historical conditions of human existence to understand what this Gospel means? Or is the Gospel addressed to man the laborer in his material struggle? Is it good news precisely because it offers divine grace in man's earthly task of creating his history? The encyclical, as we mentioned earlier, often speaks of "the Gospel of work" (nn.6, 26). A Christian theology faithful to the perspective of *Laborem exercens* must search for the "materialist" meaning of the Christian message. We recall at this point the important affirmation of the 1971 Synod of Bishops: the redemption which Jesus Christ has brought includes the liberation of men and women from the oppressive conditions of their existence.[37]

Since the teaching of the encyclical has been worked out in critical dialogue with Marxism, it is appropriate to ask whether the papal document embodies an entire philosophy or theology of history. Marxism regards itself as an interpretation of human history. It argues that history is alive by a rational dialectic, carried forward by the class struggle, which aims at the creation of a classless society freed from all alienation. Humankind will become the subject of its own history and move from the realm of necessity to the realm of freedom.

Does *Laborem exercens* present an interpretation of history? The encyclical certainly offers an interpretation of the present age. We are told that the basic contradiction of modern, industrial society is between capital and labor and that from this contradiction follow the structures of oppression and most of the world's problems. This, one will have to admit, is a Marxist perspective. Yet for Pope John Paul II there is nothing necessary here. The priority which capital holds over labor is both a structural and a moral failing. It involves sin. The great counter-force against social injustice, we are told, has been and still is the workers' movement. Again there was nothing necessary in this. For it is through solidarity, freely chosen, that workers and with them all the exploited engaged in an historical struggle for a more just society. This movement had ambiguous results, according to the encyclical. It generated two fixed ideologies, liberalism and Marxism, which blinded people to the historical reality and made them fight for the wrong ideals. At the same time, the workers' movement was successful in making capital serve labor a little more. The lot of the working people improved. Neo-capitalism emerged in Western society which held some promise. But in recent decades, the proportions of industrial exploitation have become universal in Western societies, in the communist countries, and in the third world. Against this we witness a new burst of workers' solidarity. The dynamic moment of present-day history is the struggle of the workers and the poor in general for a society in which capital can be made to serve labor. The encyclical argues that the whole of contemporary humanity has acquired the yearning of liberation, and that especially the people who until now have been burdened by great poverty and misery are waking up and become increasingly determined to struggle for their freedom, their rightful place, their share in the wealth of the earth. The forward movement of contemporary history is then the struggle of the oppressed, joined by all those who love justice.

Pope John Paul II tells the poor that God is on their side and that God is present in their struggle. We recall the remarkable sentence which says that the Church calls for solidarity *of* the poor and *with* the poor (n.8). The encyclical wants to strengthen the movements struggling for justice. As the structures of oppression have the character of sin, so do these struggles for justice embody an aspect of divine redemption.

This radical message to my mind reflects the identification of Pope John Paul II with the workers of Solidarity. The Polish Pope's solidarity with the Polish workers is the socio-political base on which the encyclical is built. This does not limit the message to the Polish context, of course. The encyclical was clearly written to shed light on the struggles in the communist world but also in capitalist society and third world countries. Yet it was during a particular moment in history, in the year 1981, when the struggle of Solidarity promised to become a turning point in Polish and possibly in European history, that a Polish Pope committed himself to radical social teaching. The struggle of Solidarity becomes the metaphor of the modern age yearning for liberation. At this moment Pope John Paul II was able to move beyond the cautious summons to reform that normally characterize papal teaching. He lifted Catholic social doctrine to a new height. He gave it a new direction.

Let us continue our inquiry. Does the encyclical move from this political and theological interpretation of modern history to an interpretation of the whole of history? Marx, we recall, did precisely this. The class conflict which characterized nineteenth century society and which he regarded as the lever for the transformation of the economic order was made by him, without adequate proof, the dynamics of universal history. The encyclical does nothing of the sort. It does not offer a theology of the historical process as such; it speaks to the modern age and its future.

One may wish to argue against my reading of the encyclical by recalling that Pope John Paul II considers man's call to become more truly subject a truly universal message. The encyclical claims that from the beginning of divine revelation it has been taught that man is defined by labor and destined to become subject (n.4). If God's gracious presence to human life has always summoned people to become subjects of their lives, analyze the obstacles to their self-responsibility, and organize a joint struggle to overcome injustice, does this not mean that there has always been in history a divine dynamics, a perpetual, ever to be renewed struggle between those who suffer injustice and those who defend the existing structures of oppression? And is this not an interpretation of world history?

The weakness of this argument is this: it is difficult to understand the repeated insistence of the encyclical that Christian teaching has never changed, that the Church has always taught that man is laborer and that man is subject and meant to become subject. Affirmations of this kind have at best a symbolic meaning; they are certainly not true literally. The biblical teaching, itself historically situated, has again and again been in dialogue with culture, and hence Church teaching has evolved and is still evolving. Christian tradition is part of history and reveals its meaning and power only in this historical process. The rich notion of subject which the encyclical employs has not, in this richness, existed prior to the modern age. It shares in the enlightenment tradition. Only when people, through scientific discoveries, technological advance and democratic structures, devised systems of communication, transportation, social change and mass production did the idea emerge that we, collectively, could assume responsibility for our history. Man as subject of history would not have had much meaning for the ancients since they lacked the tools for the remaking of society. Nor would they have known what universal solidarity was. Since their histories were still distinct and often quite separate, they had only a very limited sense of universal history. Man as subject of society, so central in the encyclical, is rooted in the biblical understanding of man, responsible and free, but in its profound and far-reaching meaning it is derived from dialogue with the enlightenment. *Laborem exercens,* I wish to argue, offers us a radical theological and political interpretation of the *contemporary* age, not an interpretation of world history. If theologians want to elaborate a theology of history, they will have to locate the advent of divine revelation and the entire Christian tradition in its own historical background and recognize the impact of labor and the laboring society in its various stages on the understanding of the Christian message.

This may be the right moment to ask how the teaching of *Laborem exercens* is related to the new movement in Christian thought called liberation theology in Latin America and political theology in Europe and North America. There are several similarities. There is also, as we shall see, a significant difference. The papal encyclical shares with liberation theology and political theology the anti-idealist, non-dualistic, labor-oriented approach to human history that might be designated as "materialist." For the encyclical and for the new theological movement man is defined as laborer, man constitutes his history through labor, and man is called upon to struggle against many obstacles to become truly the subject of his society. Secondly, *Laborem exercens* is in accord with liberation theology and political theology in its analysis of the principal cause of misery in the modern world; it is the domination of capital over labor. While they use a different vocabulary, papal teaching and liberationist theology agree that the principal source of evil in society is the master/servant relationship in the economic order, i.e., the violation of the priority of labor over capital, whether this be in the capitalist societies of the West, the communist societies of the East, or the less developed societies of the third world. For both, the struggle for a more truly human order, carried on principally by the oppressed and supported by all those who love justice, aims at making capital serve labor, at putting the wealth produced at the service of the workers, the industries, and eventually the entire laboring society. Both the encyclical and liberationist theology, turning their back on capitalism and communism, opt for a socialist vision of society, where the giant workbench at which men and women labor belongs to them and where the use of capital is determined by those who produce it. Both the encyclical and the liberationist theology have worked out their position in a critical dialogue with Marxism. Both try to transcend Marxism from within.

Laborem exercens follows what liberation theology has called "the preferential option for the poor." "The Church is firmly committed to this cause [of solidarity and struggle], for she considers it her mission, her service, a proof of her fidelity to Christ, so that she can truly be the 'Church of the poor' " (n.8). Both the encyclical and liberationist theology, then, do not approach the problems of human society from a neutral or "objective" point of view, nor do they regard human society as a complex social system in equilibrium that must be protected even if the lower sector lives in poverty. Both the encyclical and liberationist theology look at society from the point of view of the poor, the oppressed, the alienated and dependent workers. It is not an impartial but a committed approach. What becomes most visible in society from this viewpoint are the structures of oppression that introduce and multiply injustices. The common approach, then, is not only anti-idealist, non-dualistic, and labor-oriented, but it is also biased in favor of the people at the bottom.

There is, however, one important difference between the papal encyclical and the liberationist approach taken in Latin American liberation theology and European and North American political theology. This liberationist approach extends its critique not only to society and contemporary culture but also to the Church itself and the forms of ecclesiastical life. Before examining how the Church can be part of the solution, the liberationist approach asks whether the Church has been a part of the problem. Has the Church been a friend of the labor movement? Or has the Church been a friend of those who resisted these movements of solidarity? Self-critical inquiries of this sort are totally absent from *Laborem exercens*. Pope John Paul II offers much wisdom on social organization that protects the subject character of human beings, without ever asking himself whether the Catholic ecclesiastical organization corresponds to his own teaching. Do not his sharp criticism of centralization and his demand that people be co-responsible for their institutions contain a strong message for the bureaucratic structures of the Catholic Church? Because the encyclical refuses to raise any of these questions, it may lose credibility in the eyes of some readers.

A second critical remark in order at this point is the inadequate position of *Laborem exercens* on the women's movement. Despite the progress of the women's movement in the Church, the encyclical reveals a considerable insensitivity to the self-understanding of women, especially of North American women. The tone of the encyclical reflects a male world. The constant reference to "man," "his work" and "his world" is not accompanied by signs indicating that these terms have a generic meaning. When the encyclical defends a "family wage," that is to say, a remuneration for labor that allows the breadwinner and the breadwinner's family to have a decent life, the reader gets the impression that the worker in question is the male worker. At one point the English translation speaks of "the worker and his or her family" (n.8), but a glance in the official Latin text reveals that the double reference is not found there.

However what the encyclical does say about women is important. Pope John Paul II recognizes that in many countries "women work in nearly every sector of life" (n.19). One must demand that they be able to "fulfill their task in accordance with their own nature, without being discriminated against and without being excluded from jobs for which they are capable, but also without lack of respect for their family aspirations and for their specific role in contributing, together with men, to the good of society" (n.19). The encyclical insists that when women have an occupation they should be treated in such a manner that they can continue their family life and, if they so choose, become mothers. Work for women must be structured so that they retain this freedom—for instance, by granting maternity leaves. The encyclical also asks that women not be obliged to leave home and family to assume outside work, either for economic reasons or because of cultural pressures. Women have the right to stay at home and devote themselves to their families. If the wage of the husband does not suffice, then society must protect the freedom of women with the help of family allowances or grants for the labor they do at home. Pope John Paul II has a great sense that women's work at home is heavy labor. It is not only labor that builds society, it is toil. "Sometimes [women] do not receive the proper recognition on the part of society or their family for the daily burden and responsibility for their home and the upbringing of the children" (n.19).

What is missing in the encyclical is the acknowledgement of the institutionalized injustices to which women are exposed in society, culture and Church, an analysis of how this inferiorization affects women at the workplace and at home, and an inquiry into what agents in society derive benefits from these oppressive conditions. The encyclical which fully supports the labor struggle for justice and declares itself in solidarity with the poor, the marginal, and the powerless does not recognize the women's movement as a liberationist cause, a struggle for justice based on solidarity freely accorded.

Pope John Paul II's Socialism

At the conclusion of the commentary I wish to clarify precisely what economic system and social order is promoted by *Laborem exercens.* What kind of society should workers try to create? What ideals should guide Catholics in their political and social involvement?

The encyclical, as we have seen, is not an advocate of capitalism. It has chosen to give a pejorative meaning to the word "capitalism." An economic system is capitalist, we are told, even if it should call itself socialist, whenever capital has priority over labor (n.7). The encyclical recognizes that the labor movement and political power have transformed the original capitalism into "neo-capitalism," a social system that offers some assurances that the wealth produced by a nation also serves its progress and material well-being. In today's world, however, with its international connections including the third world, neo-capitalism has produced new forms of oppression. Capital again stands against the laboring people. The nationalization of the means of production, while necessary in many cases, is in and by itself not a solution. What counts is that the use of capital serve labor. To achieve this, workers, united in solidarity and joined by all who love justice, must transform the present system in two ways: (a) by introducing democracy at the workplace through workers' co-ownership, and (b) by creating a political order that allows the central planning of the economy, with international consultation. Only if decentralization and central planning protect the subject character of society can we speak of the socialization of capital.

The economic system proposed by *Laborem exercens* is a form of socialism, one in which the subject character of society is safe-guarded. As we have seen, the encyclical criticizes the existing social-ism in the Soviet bloc as centralized, authoritarian, and oppressive, as governed by a fixed ideology that is erroneous, and as violating the priority of labor over capital. In these countries, capital is not truly "socialized." Theirs is a collectivist society.

We recall at this point that papal teaching has, over the years, condemned socialism many times. Even during the great depression of the 1930's Pope Pius XI not only condemned the revolutionary communism of Russia but also the democratic socialism of the Euro-pean social-democratic parties. It was only in 1971 that the Church's official teaching changed its attitude toward socialism. In his *Octoge-sima adveniens,* Pope Paul VI recognized that many Catholics had become socialists, that they had done this as a result of their Chris-tian faith, and that by doing it they saw themselves joining the move-ment of history.[38] Who were these Catholics? One supposes that Pope Paul VI was principally thinking of Catholics joining the new forms of socialism in Africa and other parts of the third world. What did the Pope have to say to these Catholics? He drew to their atten-tion that it was necessary to distinguish between different kinds of socialism. Some of these might be in keeping with Church teaching, while others were at odds with it. He reproved forms of socialism that were wedded to a system of world interpretation or a total ideol-ogy. They easily make themselves the measure of all truth, leave no room for the worship of God, and subordinate people to the advance of their ideology. The reference was here to forms of Marxist ortho-doxies. Catholics may join socialisms that are not ideologically com-mitted. Catholics may cooperate with Marxists only if they can make sure that the Marxist ideology does not take over, only if the joint project remains pluralistic, only if there is room for different philos-ophies, including Christian faith.

It is, therefore, not altogether surprising that a papal encyclical in 1981 advocates in all frankness a particular form of socialism. How are we to characterize the socialism of Pope John Paul II?

First, Laborem exercens advocates a moral socialism. By this I mean primarily that it distinguishes itself from the so-called scientific socialism set forth by official Marxism and some other determinist versions of Marxism. From this Marxist point of view, the contradictions of capitalism are scientific; they belong to the order of socio-technology. And because they can be adequately analyzed in scientific terms, it is possible to determine scientifically the consciousness of the dominant class and culture and to define the political policy, deemed to be objectively correct, which socialists must adopt in their struggle for revolution. From this Marxist point of view, the entire language of morality and justice belongs to feudal and bourgeois culture and hence has a politically reactionary meaning.

Against this scientific or pseudo-scientific Marxism, the encyclical presents a socialism that is moral—moral from several points of view. First, the contradictions of capitalism are not only socio-technological in the sense that they will lead to the collapse of the system. They are also and especially moral, in the sense that they are due to sin, they are causes of human suffering, they push a wide sector of humanity into misery, even if the system should work well from a socio-technological point of view. Second, the socialism of *Laborem exercens* is moral because the workers' movement that brings it into being is a morally based movement: it is people in solidarity struggling for their collective self-interest in the context of the wider consideration of justice for all. The movement demands solidarity, fidelity, sacrifice, concern for others—all moral values. In particular, the Christian participation in the movement is based on faith. The Church's own identification with the workers' movement is inspired by its desire to be faithful to Jesus Christ.

One should mention in this context that the original Marxism, distinct from its determinist versions, also proposed a moral socialism.[39] For Marx, reason was not simply identified with scientific or technological reason in the contemporary sense; for Marx, reason was, with the entire enlightenment, practical reason having to do with the right order of things and hence touching upon morality. We already mentioned above that Marx's argument according to which workers are the owners of the goods they produce was an argument of practical reason; it was a moral argument. When Marx spoke of the contradictions of capitalism, he meant above all the discrepancy between the *social* nature of work in industrial society and the *private* ownership of capital. Industrial work involving the many demands ownership involving the many. This again is not an argument of scientific or technological reason but of practical reason; it has moral implications. Marx argued, moreover, that if an economic system cannot feed and house the people, then it is irrational. Again a moral reasoning. The type of reasoning we find in *Laborem exercens,* while radically at odds with scientific or positivist Marxism, has a certain affinity with the original reasoning of Marx. Both belong to the order of practical reason. The essential difference of their conclusions is this: while for Marx the ownership of capital was the great moral issue, for the encyclical, after the historical experience of over a century, it is the use of capital that really counts in the practical order.

Second, the socialism of *Laborem exercens* is liberationist. What do I mean by this? The papal teaching on socialism clearly distinguishes itself from what Marx and Engels called utopian socialism[40] and from Fabian socialism.[41] Marx and Engels polemicized against a socialism of good will, such as the Christian socialism of those days, which supposed that the preaching of virtue and the right ideas would eventually reach all members of society and result in a peaceful entry into socialism through the consensus of all. Marx and Engels argued that this utopian socialism overlooked the necessity of the workers' struggle. Utopian socialists wanted to wait until the capitalists themselves were converted to higher ideals. *Laborem exercens* does not follow this idealistic course. The encyclical, as we have seen, calls for solidarity of the workers and with the workers in the joint struggle for the priority of labor over capital. The socialist idea is here being borne to victory through the workers' movement.

The Fabian Society, the creation of a British intellectual elite at the end of the nineteenth century, presented socialism as the most rational economic system and hoped that by infiltration into various agencies of government, its members could persuasively argue for the socialist position and gradually convince the British public to accept the new orientation. The Fabians were gradualists. They were at first not linked to the labor movement at all. It was only after the creation of the Labor Party at the beginning of this century that the Fabians were drawn into the labor movement. They became the scientific advisors of the Labor Party. British (and Canadian) socialism has retained certain Fabian elements. Yet *Laborem exercens* is not Fabian;

it presents a socialism that is the result of the workers' struggle. This liberationist perspective distinguishes it from Utopian and from Fabian socialism.

Third, the socialism of the encyclical can be characterized as cooperative. It defines itself against the centralized, authoritarian collectivism of the Soviet bloc. It integrates the principles of cooperatism. The encyclical introduces cooperation on two levels. It demands, first, that the workers become co-owners and be co-responsible for the policies of their industries, and, second, that the central planning supervised by the government take place in a manner that allows for the interplay of many different institutions and local interests. It is not surprising that the encyclical dreads the idea that a government should exercise total control over the economy. As we have seen, it speaks of intermediary bodies with economic, social and cultural purposes. The economic system recommended resembles what is often called self-governing socialism,[42] except that in the encyclical the emphasis on central planning is as great as on local participation. The deep reason why the encyclical does not regard this double emphasis as a contradiction is its theological vision of man as cooperator. Labor is by its very nature cooperative. Man the laborer is a cooperator; man is made into a competitor only through special circumstances. Even the labor movement, obliged to struggle against the power of those who control capital, must be inspired by the vision of a cooperative society. Its own struggle for victory ultimately aims at cooperation. Struggling and striking workers experience an element of grief that they live in a society where struggle and strikes are necessary; they know themselves to have been created as cooperators.

Fourth, in connection with the previous point, the socialism of the encyclical has an international dimension. In the long run, because of the limitation of resources and their random distribution on the earth, it is necessary that countries that have access to many resources cooperate with countries that have few resources. Eventually the central planning in each country must take place in consultation with other countries, including the poorest regions. Only a world cooperative system ultimately deserves the name of socialism.

Fifth, the socialism recommended by the encyclical is reformist, except under unusual circumstances. The encyclical addresses itself only incidentally to the third world; it simply extends its own logic to third world countries, advocating solidarity movements with Church support. Justice may demand the radical reconstruction of society. Revolution is not excluded. But in its totality, the encyclical addresses itself to the industrialized societies of East and West. Here it takes a reformist approach. In the Eastern communist countries, the message of the encyclical is embodied in the Polish workers' movement. The existing order is to be modified by introducing democracy at the workplace and widening participation in central planning. In the Western capitalist countries, if I read the encyclical correctly, Catholics are asked to support the movements that change the existing order for the better—in other words, that move in the double direction of democracy in the industries and central planning of employment and production. In East and West workers must struggle to modify the existing systems so that capital can be made to serve labor.

Sixth, the socialism of the encyclical, while non-Marxist, is able to integrate certain Marxist paradigms. It takes Marxism seriously and is willing to learn from it, especially from the humanist and revisionist version of Marxism. We saw that the very concept of man as laborer, constituting himself through labor, is the result of an extended dialogue with Marxism. It is through the application of the personalist principle, which Pope John Paul II shared with other Polish personalists, that the encyclical widens the Marxist notions, vindicates the preeminence of the subject, and defends the subject character of society.

Finally, the encyclical proposes a non-ideological socialism. It differs from socialisms that are linked to a total philosophy of history. Ideologies, according to the definition of the encyclical, are always derived from the analysis of actual historical change; they are then abstracted from these historical circumstances and given universal validity. Ideologies are reifications. For liberalism the guiding dynamics of history is the free market; for Marxism it is class conflict. And because ideologies are abstractions, they make people believe that they can analyze new historical situations without proper attention to what is taking place. Ideologies know what is taking place before they take a look. Ideologies blind people to reality, lead them to make false analyses, and result in policies that will be harmful to all. Ideologies fail to recognize that people are subjects, and that therefore history is not scientifically predictable. By defending the openness of history, the encyclical does not present its own teaching as an ideology.

The socialism of *Laborem exercens* is non-ideological also in the sense that it recommends collaboration with any socialist movement as long as it remains open to pluralism within the common struggle. It does not occur to Pope John Paul II that a Christian movement for justice could by itself become the historical force that transforms society. What is needed is cooperation, solidarity, joint struggle. The Pope sees the Church itself in solidarity with the liberationist movement.

Is it possible to call the socialism of the encyclical itself an ideology? It is not an ideology in the sense in which the word is here defined. It does not offer a world interpretation, it does not make predictions about the future, it does not see human beings caught in a necessary logic of history that works itself out apart from the subjectivity. However, the papal teaching does offer a set of ideas and ideals that allow people to understand their historical situation, presents them with an image of what society ought to be like, and supplies them with strong motivation for the necessary struggle. Some writers call such a set of ideas and ideals an ideology. The encyclical does not. Is there a good name for an historical ideal that judges the present, guides social action and releases religious or emotional energy for the social struggle? It may be called a "utopia." This usage is derived from the revisionist Marxist philosopher, Ernst Bloch, and later was endorsed by Pope Paul VI in his *Octogesima adveniens*.[43] Utopia is here understood not as an unhistorical dream of a perfect society or a political never-never land, but as a concrete, historical social ideal, based on the potentialities of the present, that breaks with the present order, generates new social policies, and summons forth energies to struggle for the as yet unrealized possibilities of the present. Without such a "utopia," there can be no significant social change. *Laborem exercens* presents Catholics with a social utopia in this clearly defined sense.

What is the message of *Laborem exercens* for Catholics in the United States and Canada? I have made a few remarks on this topic in a previous paragraph. It seems to me that there is a radical and a reformist reading of the encyclical. If Catholics follow a radical reading, they will be overwhelmed by the judgment of the encyclical on their societies. The existing economic and political system in North America is profoundly at odds with papal teaching, nor is there a nationwide, worker-based socialist organization that struggles for the primacy of labor over capital. There seems to be no existing movement that Christians can join. The traditional parties and the trade unions are not critical enough; they seem to be reconciled to the existing order. And the tiny radical political groups that do exist have, because of their impotence, an absurdly narrow ideological commitment that makes cooperation impossible. Radical Catholics feel that they are living in the wilderness. They experience themselves as strangers in their own country. Faithful to Jesus and his message of justice and grace, they form spiritual counter-cultures, often associated with alternative life-styles. They are willing to live on the fringes of society, waiting for the moment when America will be more profoundly shaken and workers will organize their own movement for socialism.

What action does a reformist reading of the encyclical lead to? Here Catholics concentrate on the twofold direction indicated by *Laborem exercens,* namely the introduction of democracy at the workplace and the creation of a political system that allows for the rational planning of the economy. While these Catholics realize that there is no nationwide movement that serves these two ends and wrestles for the primacy of labor over capital, they think it worthwhile to engage themselves in the pursuit of one of these ends even if they only make a few steps forward. These Catholics do not fully share the wilderness experience. They are not totally overwhelmed. They are willing to engage themselves in cooperative enterprises, credit unions, workers' experiments, consumers' power, and other decentralizing citizens' initiatives; and they are willing to work with political parties or trade unions if this promises to lead to more adequate planning of production and employment and more effective protection of workers and poor people from exploitation and misery. Catholics of this kind will engage themselves in the schools and the institutions in which they work to raise the social consciousness and promote a spiritual culture at odds with capitalist society. They will do this not because they believe that their activity will usher in socialism, but because as disciples of Jesus they want to incarnate their spiritual vision in some concrete action. And if the critical people, be they radical or reformist, are faithful, who knows!—an unforeseen historical event may take place which creates social conditions, conditions in which workers will generate a mass movement to bring about the socialist society of which *Laborem exercens* speaks.

Notes

1. Cf. John Hellman, "John Paul II and the Personalist Movement," *Cross Currents,* 30 (Winter 1980–81) 409–419.

2. In his first encyclical, *Redemptor hominis,* n. 15, Pope John Paul II advocated a planned economy. For an analysis see G. Baum, "A Pope from the Second World," *The Ecumenist,* 18 (Jan.–Feb. 1980), p. 25.

3. Cf. Pope John Paul II's address to the United Nations (1979), n. 18.

4. For the papal teaching on socialism see G. Baum, *Catholics and Canadian Socialism,* Paulist Press, New York, 1980, pp. 71–96.

5. *Quadragesimo anno,* n. 109. See Baum, *op. cit.,* p. 81.

6. *Pacem in terris,* n. 159. See Baum, *op. cit.,* p. 88.

7. *Octogesima adveniens,* n. 30. See Baum, *op. cit.,* p. 88.

8. *Ibid.,* n. 31.

9. Marx affirms man's self-constitution through labor against Feuerbach's idealism. Cf. Marx's "Theses on Feuerbach," and his *The German Ideology.* It is not my intention in this commentary to offer detailed references to Marx's work. Instead I ask the reader to consult A. McGovern, *Marxism: An American Christian Perspective,* Orbis Books, Maryknoll, N.Y., which gives an introduction to Marx's work and the debates among his commentators.

10. Cf. G. Baum, *Religion and Alienation,* Paulist Press, New York, 1975, pp. 24–30.

11. Marx developed his earliest notion of human emancipation in his essays, "On the Jewish Question." Cf. A. McGovern, *op. cit.,* p. 20.

12. Cf. A. McGovern, *op. cit.,* p. 24.

13. *Ibid.,* pp. 32–33, 68–82.

14. Speaking before the United Nations, Pope John Paul II stressed the impact of structures upon consciousness and society. "The roots of hatred, destruction and contempt are not so much in the hearts of the nations as in

the inner determinations of the systems that decide the history of whole societies" (n. 11). And speaking at Yankee Stadium, the Pope said, "Within the framework of your national institutions and in cooperation with all your compatriots you will also want to seek out the structural reasons which foster or cause the different forms of poverty in the world and in your own country" (n. 4). See G. Baum, "A Pope from the Second World," pp. 24–25.

15. See especially Marx's essays, "Wages of Labor" and "Profit of Capital" in his *Economic and Philosophical Manuscripts.*

16. Cf. A. McGovern, *op. cit.,* pp. 32–33, 68–82.

17. *Populorum progressio,* nn. 29–32.

18. Cf. G. Baum, *Catholics and Canadian Socialism,* pp. 71–81.

19. *Quadragesimo anno,* n. 114.

20. For an analysis, see G. Baum, "A Pope from the Second World," pp. 24–25.

21. Cf. Harry Boyte, *The Backyard Revolution,* Temple, Philadelphia, 1980.

22. See Marx's essays "On the Jewish Question."

23. See Marx's essay "Alienated Labor" in his *Economic and Philosophical Manuscripts.* Cf. A. McGovern, *op. cit.,* p. 28.

24. In *Redemptor hominis,* nn. 15–16, Pope John Paul argues that in a world of scarcity the production and distribution of goods must be responsibly planned. He speaks of a planning that is "rational and honest" and "long-range and authentically human."

25. Cf. B. Baum, *Catholics and Canadian Socialism,* pp. 89–90.

26. John Mihevc, "Religion in Yugoslavia," *The Ecumenist,* 17 (July–Aug. 1979), pp. 68–71.

27. P. Vaillancourt, "Nicaragua: Living a Revolution," *The Ecumenist,* 19 (Sept.–Oct. 1981), pp. 88–90.

28. *Redemptor hominis,* n. 15. See Baum, "A Pope from the Second World," p. 24.

29. Cf. G. Baum, *Religion and Alienation,* pp. 54–55.

30. Cf. G. Baum, "Peter Berger's Unfinished Symphony," in *Sociology and Human Destiny,* ed. G. Baum, Seabury, New York, 1980, pp. 121–123.

31. Jacques Ellul, *The Technological Society,* Vintage Books, New York, 1967.

32. Dona Palmer *et al.,* "A Call to Life: U.S. Catholic Response to the Arms Race," *The Ecumenist,* 20 (Jan.–Feb., 1982).

33. *Quadragesimo anno,* n. 106.

34. Cf. "The Biblical Interpretation of Nature and Human Dominion," *Faith, Science and the Future,* Church and Society, W.C.C., Geneva, Switzerland, 1979, pp. 40–43.

35. Already in his first encyclical, *Redemptor hominis,* Pope John Paul II proposed a theory of the primacy of the spiritual which, in a commentary, I interpreted to mean "concrete spirit." Spirit is always empowerment to act in the world. Cf. G. Baum, "The First Papal Encyclical," *The Ecumenist,* 17 (May–June 1979), pp. 56–57.

36. In a previous ecclesiastical document, a pastoral declaration on Euro-Communism by the French bishops, we find a similar non-dualist, anti-idealist approach. The declaration mentions that Marx discovered the impact of labor on consciousness. In my commentary on this document I wrote: "The 'materialism' which sees man as organizing his labor and in doing so creating his own consciousness is, therefore, not at odds with the Christian vision as long as the materialist perspective is completed by the recognition that in this process of acting and thinking a transcendent divine mystery is at work, calling and empowering men and women toward the horizon of freedom and reconciliation": G. Baum, *The Social Imperative,* Paulist Press, New York, 1978, p. 201.

37. "Justice in the World," n. 6.

38. *Octogesima adveniens,* n.31.

39. Cf. A. McGovern, *op. cit.,* pp. 32–34.

40. Cf. F. Engels, "Socialism: Utopian and Scientific," *The Marxists,* ed. C. Wright Mills, New York, 1962, pp. 72–80.

41. Cf. G. Baum, *Catholics and Canadian Socialism,* pp. 44–46.

42. Cf. *Self-Governing Socialism: A Reader,* ed. by B. Horvat *et al.,* 2 vols., International Arts and Sciences Press, White Plains, N.Y., 1975.

43. *Octogesima adveniens,* n. 37. Cf. G. Baum, "Debate over Utopia," *The Ecumenist,* 18 (May–June 1980), pp. 60–64.

APPENDIX:
Laborem exercens

Encyclical Letter of Pope John Paul II

*(1) provision
(2) contribution
to society
community)*

Through work man must earn his daily bread[1] and contribute to the continual advance of science and technology and, above all, to elevating unceasingly the cultural and moral level of the society within which he lives in community with those who belong to the same family. And work means any activity by man, whether manual or intellectual, whatever its nature or circumstances; it means any human activity that can and must be recognized as work, in the midst of all the many activities of which man is capable and to which he is predisposed by his very nature, by virtue of humanity itself. Man is made to be in the visible universe an image and likeness of God himself,[2] and he is placed in it in order to subdue the earth.[3] From the beginning therefore he is called to work. Work is one of the characteristics that distinguish man from the rest of creatures, whose activity for sustaining their lives cannot be called work. Only man is capable of work, and only man works, at the same time by work occupying his existence on earth. Thus work bears a particular mark of man and of humanity, the mark of a person operating within a community of persons. And this mark decides its interior characteristics; in a sense it constitutes its very nature.

I. INTRODUCTION

1. Human Work on the Ninetieth Anniversary of "Rerum Novarum"

Since May 15 of the present year was the ninetieth anniversary of the publication by the great Pope of the "social question," Leo XIII, of the decisively important encyclical which begins with the words "Rerum novarum," I wish to devote this document to human work and, even more, to man in the vast context of the reality of work. As I said in the encyclical "Redemptor Hominis," published at the beginning of my service in the See of St. Peter in Rome, man "is the primary and fundamental way for the Church,"[4] precisely because of the inscrutable mystery of redemption in Christ; and so it is necessary to return constantly to this way and to follow it ever anew in the various aspects in which it shows us all the wealth and at the same time all the toil of human existence on earth.

Work is one of these aspects, a perennial and fundamental one, one that is always relevant and constantly demands renewed attention and decisive witness. Because fresh questions and problems are always arising, there are always fresh hopes, but also fresh fears and threats connected with this basic dimension of human existence. Man's life is built up every day from work, from work it derives its specific dignity, but at the same time work contains the unceasing measure of human toil and suffering and also of the harm and injustice which penetrate deeply into social life within individual nations and on the international level. While it is true that man eats the bread produced by the work of his hands[5]—and this means not only the daily bread by which his body keeps alive but also the bread of science and progress, civilization and culture—it is also a perennial truth that he eats this bread by "the sweat of his face,"[6] that is to say, not only by personal effort and toil, but also in the midst of many tensions, conflicts and crises, which in relationship with the reality of work disturb the life of individual societies and also of all humanity.

We are celebrating the ninetieth anniversary of the encyclical "Rerum Novarum" on the eve of new developments in technological, economic and political conditions which, according to many experts, will influence the world of work and production no less than the industrial revolution of the last century. There are many factors of a general nature; the widespread introduction of automation into many spheres of production, the increase in the cost of energy and raw materials, the growing realization that the heritage of nature is limited and that it is being intolerably polluted, and the emergence on the political scene of peoples who, after centuries of subjection, are demanding their rightful place among the nations and in international decision making. These new conditions and demands will require a reordering and adjustment of the structures of the modern economy and of the distribution of work. Unfortunately, for millions of skilled workers these changes may perhaps mean unemployment, at least for a time, or the need for retraining. They will very probably involve a reduction or a less rapid increase in material well-being for the more developed countries. But they can also bring relief and hope to the millions who today live in conditions of shameful and unworthy poverty.

It is not for the Church to analyze scientifically the consequences that these changes may have on human society. But the Church considers it to be its task always to call attention to the dignity and rights of those who work, to condemn situations in which that dignity and those rights are violated, and to help to guide the above-mentioned changes so as to ensure authentic progress by man and society.

2. In the Organic Development of the Church's Social Action and Teaching

It is certainly true that work as a human issue is at the very center of the "social question" to which, for almost a hundred years since the publication of the above-mentioned encyclical, the Church's teaching and the many undertakings connected with its apostolic mission have been especially directed. The present reflections on work are not intended to follow a different line, but rather to be in organic connection with the whole tradition of this teaching and activity. At the same time, however, I am making them, according to the indication in the Gospel, in order to bring out from the heritage of the Gospel "what is new and what is old."[7] Certainly work is part of "what is old"—as old as man and his life on earth.

Nevertheless, the general situation of man in the modern world, studied and analyzed in its various aspects of geography, culture and civilization, calls for the discovery of the new meanings of human work. It likewise calls for the formulation of the new tasks that in this sector face each individual, the family, each country, the whole human race and finally the Church itself.

During the years that separate us from the publication of the encyclical "Rerum Novarum," the social question has not ceased to engage the Church's attention. Evidence of this are the many documents of the magisterium issued by the Popes and by the Second Vatican Council, pronouncements by individual episcopates, and the activity of the various centers of thought and of practical apostolic initiatives, both on the international level and at the level of the local churches. It is difficult to list here in detail all the manifestations of the commitment of the Church and of Christians in the social question, for they are too numerous. As a result of the Council, the main coordinating center in this field is the Pontifical Commission on Justice and Peace, which has corresponding bodies within the individual bishops' conferences. The name of this institution is very significant. It indicates that the social question must be dealt with in its whole complex dimension. Commitment to justice must be closely linked with commitment to peace in the modern world. This twofold commitment is certainly supported by the painful experience of the two great world wars which in the course of the last ninety years have convulsed many European countries and, at least partially, countries in other continents. It is supported, especially since World War II, by the permanent threat of a nuclear war and the prospect of the terrible self-destruction that emerges from it.

If we follow the main line of development of the documents of the supreme magisterium of the Church, we find in them an explicit confirmation of precisely such a statement of the question. The key position, as regards the question of world peace, is that of John XXIII's encyclical "Pacem in Terris." However, if one studies the development of the question of social justice, one cannot fail to note that, whereas during the period between "Rerum Novarum" and Pius XI's "Quadragesimo Anno" the Church's teaching concentrates mainly on the just solution of the "labor question" within individual nations, in the next period the Church's teaching widens its horizon to take in the whole world. The disproportionate distribution of wealth and poverty and the existence of some countries and continents that are developed and of others that are not call for a leveling out and for a search for ways to ensure just development for all. This is the direction of the teaching in John XXIII's encyclical "Mater et Magistra," in the pastoral constitution "Gaudium et Spes" of the Second Vatican Council and in Paul VI's encyclical "Populorum Progressio."

This trend of development of the Church's teaching and commitment in the social question exactly corresponds to the objective recognition of the state of affairs. While in the past the "class" question was especially highlighted as the center of this issue, in more recent times it is the "world" question that is emphasized. Thus, not only the sphere of class is taken into consideration, but also the world sphere of inequality and injustice and, as a consequence, not only the class dimension, but also the world dimension of the tasks involved in the path toward the achievement of justice in the modern world. A complete analysis of the situation of the world today shows in an even deeper and fuller way the meaning of the previous analysis of social injustices; and it is the meaning that must be given today to efforts to build justice on earth, not concealing thereby unjust structures, but demanding that they be examined and transformed on a more universal scale.

3. The Question of Work as the Key to the Social Question

In the midst of all these processes—those of the diagnosis of objective social reality and also those of the Church's teaching in the sphere of the complex and many-sided social question—the question of human work naturally appears many times. This issue is, in a way, a constant factor both of social life and of the Church's teaching. Furthermore, in this teaching attention to the question goes back much further than the last ninety years. In fact the Church's social teaching finds it source in Sacred Scripture, beginning with the Book of Genesis and especially in the Gospels and the writings of the apostles. From the beginning it was part of the Church's teaching, its concept of man and life in society, and especially the social morality which it worked out according to the needs of the different ages. This traditional patrimony was then inherited and developed by the teaching of the Popes on the modern "social question," beginning with the encyclical "Rerum Novarum." In this context, study of the question of work, as we have seen, has continually been brought up to date while maintaining that Christian basis of truth which can be called ageless.

While in the present document we return to this question once more—without however any intention of touching on all the topics that concern it—this is not merely in order to gather together and repeat what is already contained in the Church's teaching. It is rather in order to highlight—perhaps more than has been done before—the fact that human work is a key, probably the essential key, to the whole social question, if we try to see the question really from the point of view of man's good. And if the solution—or rather the gradual solution—of the social question, which keeps coming up and becomes ever more complex, must be sought in the direction of "making life more human,"[8] then the key, namely human work, acquires fundamental and decisive importance.

II. WORK AND MAN

4. In the Book of Genesis

The Church is convinced that work is a fundamental dimension of man's existence on earth. It is confirmed in this conviction by considering the whole heritage of the many sciences devoted to man: anthropology, paleontology, history, sociology, psychology, and so on; they all seem to bear witness to this reality in an irrefutable way. But the source of the Church's conviction is above all the revealed word of God, and therefore what is a conviction of the intellect is also a conviction of faith. The reason is that the Church—and it is worthwhile stating it at this point—believes in man; it thinks of man and addresses itself to him not only in the light of historical experience, not only with the aid of the many methods of scientific knowledge, but in the first place in the light of the revealed word of the living God. Relating itself to man, it seeks to express the eternal designs and transcendent destiny, which the living God, the Creator and Redeemer, has linked with him.

The Church finds in the very first pages of the Book of Genesis the source of its conviction that work is a fundamental dimension of human existence on earth. An analysis of these texts makes us aware that they express—sometimes in an archaic way of manifesting thought—the fundamental truths about man, in the context of the mystery of creation itself. These truths are decisive for man from the very beginning, and at the same time they trace out the main lines of his earthly existence, both in the state of original justice and also after the breaking, caused by sin, of the Creator's original covenant with creation in man. When man, who had been created "in the image of God . . . male and female,"[9] hears the words: "Be fruitful and multiply, and fill the earth and subdue it,"[10] even though these words do not refer directly and explicitly to work, beyond any doubt they indirectly indicate it as an activity for man to carry out in the world. Indeed, they show its very deepest essence. Man is the image of God partly through the mandate received from his Creator to subdue, to dominate, the earth. In carrying out this mandate, man, every human being, reflects the very action of the Creator of the universe.

Work understood as a "transitive" activity, that is to say, an activity beginning in the human subject and directed toward an external object, presupposes a specific dominion by man over "the earth," and in its turn it confirms and develops this dominion. It is clear that the term "the earth" of which the biblical text speaks is to be understood in the first place as that fragment of the visible universe that man inhabits. By extension, however, it can be understood as the whole of the visible world insofar as it comes within the range of man's influence and of his striving to satisfy his needs. The expression "subdue the earth" has an immense range. It means all the resources that the earth (and indirectly the visible world) contains and which, through the conscious activity of man, can be discovered and used for his ends. And so these words, placed at the beginning of the Bible, never cease to be relevant. They embrace equally the past ages of civilization and economy, as also the whole of modern reality and future phases of development, which are perhaps already to some extent beginning to take shape, though for the most part they are still almost unknown to man and hidden from him.

While people sometimes speak of periods of "acceleration" in the economic life and civilization of humanity or of individual nations, linking these periods to the progress of science and technology and especially to discoveries which are decisive for social and economic life, at the same time it can be said that none of these phenomena of "acceleration" exceeds the essential content of what was said in that most ancient of biblical texts. As man, through his work, becomes more and more the master of the earth, and as he confirms his dominion over the visible world, again through his work, he nevertheless remains in every case and at every phase of this process within the Creator's original ordering. And this ordering remains necessarily and indissolubly linked with the fact that man was created, as male and female, "in the image of God." This process is, at the same time, universal: It embraces all human beings, every generation, every phase of economic and cultural development, and at the same time it is a process that takes place within each human being, in each conscious human subject. Each and every individual is at the same time embraced by it. Each and every individual, to the proper extent and in an incalculable number of ways, takes part in the giant process whereby man "subdues the earth" through his work.

5. Work in the Objective Sense: Technology

This universality and, at the same time, this multiplicity of the process of "subduing the earth" throw light upon human work, because man's dominion over the earth is achieved in and by means of work. There thus emerges the meaning of work in an objective sense, which finds expression in the various epochs of culture and civilization. Man dominates the earth by the very fact of domesticating animals, rearing them and obtaining from them the food and clothing he needs, and by the fact of being able to extract various natural resources from the earth and the seas. But man "subdues the earth" much more when he begins to cultivate it and then to transform its products, adapting them to his own use. Thus agriculture constitutes through human work a primary field of economic activity and an indispensable factor of production. Industry in its turn will always consist in linking the earth's riches—whether nature's living resources, or the products of agriculture, or the mineral or chemical resources—with man's work, whether physical or intellectual. This is also in a sense true in the sphere of what are called service industries as well as in the sphere of research, pure or applied.

In industry and agriculture man's work has today in many cases ceased to be mainly manual, for the toil of human hands and muscles is aided by more and more highly perfected machinery. Not only in industry but also in agriculture we are witnessing the transformations made possible by the gradual development of science and technology. Historically speaking this, taken as a whole, has caused great changes in civilization, from the beginning of the "industrial era" to the successive phases of development through new technologies, such as the electronics and the microprocessor technology in recent years.

While it may seem that in the industrial process it is the machine that "works" and man merely supervises it, making it function and keeping it going in various ways, it is also true that for this very reason industrial development provides grounds for reproposing in new ways the question of human work. Both the original industrialization that gave rise to what is called the worker question and the subsequent industrial and post-industrial changes show in an eloquent manner that, even in the age of ever more mechanized "work," the proper subject of work continues to be man.

The development of industry and of the various sectors connected with it, even the most modern electronics technology, especially in the fields of miniaturization, communications and telecommunications and so forth, shows how vast is the role of technology, that ally of work that human thought has produced in the interaction between the subject and object of work (in the widest sense of the word). Understood in this case not as a capacity or aptitude for work, but rather as a whole set of instruments which man uses in his work, technology is undoubtedly man's ally. It facilitates his work, perfects, accelerates and augments it. It leads to an increase in the quantity of things produced by work and in many cases improves their quality. However it is also a fact that in some instances technology can cease to be man's ally and become almost his enemy, as when the mechanization of work "supplants" him, taking away all personal satisfaction and the incentive to creativity and responsibility, when it deprives many workers of their previous employment or when, through exalting the machine, it reduces man to the status of its slave.

If the biblical words "subdue the earth" addressed to man from the very beginning are understood in the context of the whole modern age, industrial and post-industrial, then they undoubtedly include also a relationship with technology, with the world of machinery which is the fruit of the work of the human intellect and an historical confirmation of man's dominion over nature.

The recent stage of human history, especially that of certain societies, brings a correct affirmation of technology as a basic co-efficient of economic progress; but at the same time this affirmation has been accompanied by and continues to be accompanied by essential questions concerning human work in relationship to its subject, which is man. These questions are particularly charged with content and tension of an ethical and an ethical and social character. They therefore constitute a continual challenge for institutions of many kinds, for states and governments, for systems and international organizations; they also constitute a challenge for the Church.

6. Work in the Subjective Sense: Man as the Subject of Work

In order to continue our analysis of work, an analysis linked with the word of the Bible telling man that he is to subdue the earth, we must concentrate our attention on work in the subjective sense, much more than we did on the objective significance, barely touching upon the vast range of problems known intimately and in detail to scholars in various fields and also, according to their specializations, to those who work. If the words of the Book of Genesis to which we refer in this analysis of ours speak of work in the objective sense in an indirect way, they also speak only indirectly of the subject of work; but what they say is very eloquent and is full of great significance.

Man has to subdue the earth and dominate, because as the "image of God" he is a person, that is to say, a subjective being capable of acting in a planned and rational way, capable of deciding about himself and with a tendency to self-realization. As a person, man is therefore the subject of work. As a person he works; he performs various actions belonging to the work process. Independently of their objective content, these actions must all serve to realize his humanity, to fulfill the calling to be a person that is his by reason of his very humanity. The principal truths concerning this theme were recently recalled by the Second Vatican Council in the Constitution "Gaudium et Spes," especially in Chapter 1, which is devoted to man's calling.

And so this "dominion" spoken of in the biblical text being meditated upon here not only refers to the objective dimension of work, but at the same time introduces us to an understanding of its subjective dimension. Understood as a process whereby man and the human race subdue the earth, work corresponds to this basic biblical concept only when throughout the process man manifests himself and confirms himself as the one who "dominates." This dominion, in a certain sense, refers to the subjective dimension even more than to the objective one. This dimension conditions the very ethical nature of work. In fact there is no doubt that human work has a ethical value of its own, which clearly and directly remains linked to the fact that the one who carries it out is a person, a conscious and free subject, that is to say, a subject who decides about himself.

This truth, which in a sense constitutes the fundamental and perennial heart of Christian teaching on human work, has had and continues to have primary significance for the formulation of the important social problems characterizing whole ages.

The ancient world introduced its own typical differentiation of people into classes according to the type of work done. Work which demanded from the worker the exercise of physical strength, the work of muscles and hands, was considered unworthy of free men and was therefore given to slaves. By broadening certain aspects that already belonged to the Old Testament, Christianity brought about a fundamental change of ideas in this field, taking the whole content of the Gospel message as its point of departure, especially the fact that the one who, while being God, became like us in all things[11] devoted most of the years of his life on earth to manual work at the carpenter's bench. This circumstance constitutes in itself the most eloquent "gospel of work," showing that the basis for determining the value of human work is not primarily the kind of work being done, but the

what about the certain types of effects of work on the person

fact that the one who is doing it is a person. The sources of the dignity of work are to be sought primarily in the subjective dimension, not in the objective one.

Such a concept practically does away with the very basis of the ancient differentiation of people into classes according to the kind of work done. This does not mean that from the objective point of view human work cannot and must not be rated and qualified in any way. It only means that the primary basis of the value of work is man himself, who is its subject. This leads immediately to a very important conclusion of an ethical nature: However true it may be that man is destined for work and called to it, in the first place work is "for man" and not man "for work." Through this conclusion one rightly comes to recognize the preeminence of the subjective meaning of work over the objective one. Given this way of understanding things and presupposing that different sorts of work that people do can have greater or lesser objective value, let us try nevertheless to show that each sort is judged above all by the measure of the dignity of the subject of work, that is to say, the person, the individual who carries it out. On the other hand, independent of the work that every man does, and presupposing that this work constitutes a purpose—at times a very demanding one—of his activity, this purpose does not possess a definitive meaning in itself. In fact, in the final analysis it is always man who is the purpose of the work, whatever work it is that is done by man—even if the common scale of values rates it as the merest "service," as the most monotonous, even the most alienating work.

7. A Threat to the Right Order of Values

It is precisely these fundamental affirmations about work that always emerged from the wealth of Christian truth, especially from the very message of the "gospel of work," thus creating the basis for a new way of thinking, judging and acting. In the modern period, from the beginning of the industrial age, the Christian truth about work had to oppose the various trends of materialistic and economistic thought.

For certain supporters of such ideas, work was understood and treated as a sort of "merchandise" that the worker—especially the

A problem w/ viewing work as a commodity

industrial worker—sells to the employer, who at the same time is the possessor of the capital, that is to say, of all the working tools and means that make production possible. This way of looking at work was widespread especially in the first half of the nineteenth century. Since then explicit expressions of this sort have almost disappeared and have given way to more human ways of thinking about work and evaluating it. The interaction between the worker and the tools and means of production has given rise to the development of various forms of capitalism—parallel with various forms of collectivism—into which other socio-economic elements have entered as a consequence of new concrete circumstances, of the activity of workers' associations and public authorities, and of the emergence of large transnational enterprises. Nevertheless, the danger of treating work as a special kind of "merchandise" or as an impersonal "force" needed for production (the expression "work force" is in fact in common use) always exists, especially when the whole way of looking at the question of economics is marked by the premises of materialistic economism.

A systematic opportunity for thinking and evaluating in this way, and in a certain sense a stimulus for doing so, is provided by the quickening process of the development of a one-sidedly materialistic civilization, which gives prime importance to the objective dimension of work, while the subjective dimension—everything in direct or indirect relationship with the subject of work—remains on a secondary level. In all cases of this sort, in every social situation of this type, there is a confusion or even a reversal of the order laid down from the beginning by the words of the Book of Genesis: Man is treated as an instrument of production,[12] whereas he—he alone, independent of the work he does—ought to be treated as the effective subject of work and its true maker and creator. Precisely this reversal of order, whatever the program or name under which it occurs, should rightly be called "capitalism"—in the sense more fully explained below. Everybody knows that capitalism has a definite historical meaning as a system, an economic and social system, opposed to "socialism" or "communism." But in the light of the analysis of the fundamental reality of the whole economic process—first and foremost of the production structures that work it—it should be recognized that the error of early capitalism can be repeated wherever man is in a way treated on the same level as the whole complex of the material means of production, as an instrument and not in accordance with the true dignity of his work—that is to say, where he is not treated as subject and maker, and for this very reason as the true purpose of the whole process of production.

This explains why the analysis of human work in the light of the words concerning man's "dominion" over the earth goes to the very heart of the ethical and social question. This concept should also find a central place in the whole sphere of social and economic policy, both within individual countries and in the wider field of international and intercontinental relationships, particularly with reference to the tensions making themselves felt in the world not only between East and West but also between North and South. But John XXIII in the encyclical "Mater et Magistra" and Paul VI in the encyclical "Populorum Progressio" gave special attention to these dimensions of the modern ethical and social question.

8. Worker Solidarity

When dealing with human work in the fundamental dimension of its subject, that is to say, the human person doing the work, one must make at least a summary evaluation of developments during the ninety years since "Rerum Novarum" in relation to the subjective dimension of work. Although the subject of work is always the same, that is to say man, nevertheless wide-ranging changes take place in the objective aspect. While one can say that, by reason of its subject, work is one single thing (one and unrepeatable every time), yet when one takes into consideration its objective directions one is forced to admit that there exist many works, many different sorts of work. The development of human civilization brings continual enrichment in this field. But at the same time, one cannot fail to note that in the process of this development not only do new forms of work appear but also others disappear. Even if one accepts that on the whole this is a normal phenomenon, it must still be seen whether certain ethically and socially dangerous irregularities creep in and to what extent.

It was precisely one such wide-ranging anomaly that gave rise in the last century to what has been called "the worker question," sometimes described as "the proletariat question." This question and the problems connected with it gave rise to a just social reaction and caused the impetuous emergence of a great burst of solidarity between workers, first and foremost industrial workers. The call to solidarity and common action addressed to the workers—especially to those engaged in narrowly specialized, monotonous and depersonalized work in industrial plants, when the machine tends to dominate man—was important and eloquent from the point of view of social ethics. It was the reaction against the degradation of man as the subject of work and against the unheard-of accompanying exploitation in the field of wages, working conditions and social security for the worker. The reaction united the working world in a community marked by great solidarity.

Following the lines laid down by the encyclical "Rerum Novarum" and many later documents of the Church's magisterium, it must be frankly recognized that the reaction against the system of injustice and harm that cried to heaven for vengeance[13] and that weighed heavily upon workers in that period of rapid industrialization was justified from the point of view of social morality. This state of affairs was favored by the liberal socio-political system, which in accordance with its "economistic" premises, strengthened and safeguarded economic initiative by the possessors of capital alone, but did not pay sufficient attention to the rights of the workers, on the grounds that human work is solely an instrument of production, and that capital is the basis, efficient factor and purpose of production.

From that time, worker solidarity, together with a cleaner and more committed realization by others of workers' rights, has in many cases brought about profound changes. Various forms of neo-capitalism or collectivism have developed. Various new systems have been thought out. Workers can often share in running businesses and in controlling their productivity, and in fact do so. Through appropriate associations they exercise influence over conditions of work and pay, and also over social legislation. But at the same time various ideological or power systems and new relationships which have arisen at various levels of society have allowed flagrant injustices to persist or have created new ones. On the world level, the develop-

ment of civilization and of communications has made possible a
more complete diagnosis of the living and working conditions of man
globally, but it has also revealed other forms of injustice much more
extensive than those which in the last century stimulated unity between workers for particular solidarity in the working world. This is
true in countries which have completed a certain process of industrial revolution. It is also true in countries where the main working mi-
lieu continues to be agriculture or other similar occupations.

Movements of solidarity in the sphere of work—a solidarity that
must never mean being closed to dialogue and collaboration with
others—can be necessary also with reference to the condition of social groups that were not previously included in such movements,
but which in changing social systems and conditions of living are undergoing what is in effect "proletarianization" or which actually already find themselves in a "proletariat" situation, one which, even if
not yet given that name, in fact deserves it. This can be true of certain categories or groups of the working "intelligentsia," especially
when ever wider access to education and an ever increasing number
of people with degrees or diplomas in the fields of their cultural preparation are accompanied by a drop in demand for their labor. This
unemployment of intellectuals occurs or increases when the education available is not oriented toward the types of employment or service required by the true needs of society, or when there is less
demand for work which requires education, at least professional education, than for manual labor, or when it is less well paid. Of course,
education in itself is always valuable and an important enrichment of
the human person; but in spite of that, "proletarianization" processes
remain possible.

For this reason there must be continued study of the subject of
work and of the subject's living conditions. In order to achieve social
justice in the various parts of the world, in the various countries and
in the relationships between them, there is a need for ever new movements of solidarity of the workers and with the workers. This solidarity must be present whenever it is called for by the social
degrading of the subject of work, by exploitation of the workers and
by the growing areas of poverty and even hunger. The Church is
firmly committed to this cause, for it considers it to be its mission, its

service, a proof of its fidelity to Christ, so that it can truly be the "Church of the poor." And the "poor" appear under various forms; they appear in various places and at various times; in many cases they appear as a result of the violation of the dignity of human work: either because the opportunities for human work are limited as a result of the scourge of unemployment or because a low value is put on work and the rights that flow from it, especially the right to a just wage and to the personal security of the worker and his or her family.

9. Work and Personal Dignity

Remaining within the context of man as the subject of work, it is now appropriate to touch upon, at least in a summary way, certain problems that more closely define the dignity of human work in that they make it possible to characterize more fully its specific moral value. In doing this we must always keep in mind the biblical calling to "subdue the earth,"[14] in which is expressed the will of the Creator that work should enable man to achieve that "dominion" in the visible world that is proper to him.

God's fundamental and original intention with regard to man, whom he created in his image and after his likeness,[15] was not withdrawn or canceled out even when man, having broken the original covenant with God, heard the words: "In the sweat of your face you shall eat bread."[16] These words refer to the sometimes heavy toil that from then onward has accompanied human work; but they do not alter the fact that work is the means whereby man achieves that "dominion" which is proper to him over the visible world, by "subjecting" the earth. Toil is something that is universally known, for it is universally experienced. It is familiar to those doing physical work under sometimes exceptionally laborious conditions. It is familiar not only to agricultural workers, who spend long days working the land, which sometimes "bears thorns and thistles,"[17] but also to those who work in mines and quarries, to steelworkers at their blast furnaces, to those who work in builders' yards and in construction work, often in danger of injury or death. It is also familiar to those at an intellectual workbench; to scientists; to those who bear the burden of grave responsibility for decisions that will have a vast impact on society. It is familiar to doctors and nurses, who spend days and nights at their patients' bedside. It is familiar to women, who sometimes without proper recognition on the part of society and even of their own families bear the daily burden and responsibility for their homes and the upbringing of their children. It is familiar to all workers and, since work is a universal calling, it is familiar to everyone.

And yet in spite of all this toil—perhaps, in a sense, because of it—work is a good thing for man. Even though it bears the mark of a "bonum arduum," in the terminology of St. Thomas,[18] this does not take away the fact that, as such, it is a good thing for man. It is not only good in the sense that it is useful or something to enjoy; it is also good as being something worthy, that is to say, something that corresponds to man's dignity, that expresses this dignity and increases it. If one wishes to define more clearly the ethical meaning of work, it is this truth that one must particularly keep in mind. Work is a good thing for man—a good thing for his humanity—because through work man not only transforms nature, adapting it to his own needs, but he also achieves fulfillment as a human being and indeed in a sense becomes "more a human being."

Without this consideration it is impossible to understand the meaning of the virtue of industriousness, and more particularly it is impossible to understand why industriousness should be a virtue. For virtue, as a moral habit, is something whereby man becomes good as man.[19] This fact in no way alters our justifiable anxiety that in work, whereby matter gains in nobility, man himself should not experience a lowering of his own dignity.[20] Again, it is well known that it is possible to use work in various ways against man, that it is possible to punish man with the system of forced labor in concentration camps, that work can be made into a means for oppressing man, and that in various ways it is possible to exploit human labor, that is to say, the workers. All this pleads in favor of the moral obligation to link industriousness as a virtue with the social order of work, which will enable man to become in work "more a human being" and not be degraded by it not only because of the wearing out of his physical strength (which, at least up to a certain point, is inevitable), but especially through damage to the dignity and subjectivity that are proper to him.

10. Work and Society: Family and Nation

Having thus confirmed the personal dimension of human work, we must go on to the second sphere of values which is necessarily linked to work. Work constitutes a foundation for the formation of family life, which is a natural right and something that man is called to. These two spheres of values—one linked to work and the other consequent on the family nature of human life—must be properly united and must properly permeate each other. In a way, work is a condition for making it possible to found a family, since the family requires the means of subsistence which man normally gains through work. Work and industriousness also influence the whole process of education in the family, for the very reason that everyone "becomes a human being" through, among other things, work, and becoming a human being is precisely the main purpose of the whole process of education. Obviously, two aspects of work in a sense come into play here: the one making family life and its upkeep possible, and the other making possible the achievement of the purposes of the family, especially education. Nevertheless, these two aspects of work are linked to one another and are mutually complementary in various points.

It must be remembered and affirmed that the family constitutes one of the most important terms of reference for shaping the social and ethical order of human work. The teaching of the Church has always devoted special attention to this question, and in the present document we shall have to return to it. In fact, the family is simultaneously a community made possible by work and the first school of work, within the home, for every person.

The third sphere of values that emerges from this point of view—that of the subject of work—concerns the great society to which man belongs on the basis of particular cultural and historical links. This society—even when it has not yet taken on the mature form of a nation—is not only the great "educator" of every man, even though an indirect one (because each individual absorbs within the family the contents and values that go to make up the culture of a given nation); it is also a great historical and social incarnation of the work of all generations. All of this brings it about that man combines his deepest human identity with membership of a nation, and intends his work also to increase the common good developed together with his compatriots, thus realizing that in this way work serves to add to the heritage of the whole human family, of all the people living in the world.

These three spheres are always important for human work in its subjective dimension. And this dimension, that is to say, the concrete reality of the worker, takes precedence over the objective dimension. In the subjective dimension there is realized, first of all, that "dominion" over the world of nature to which man is called from the beginning according to the words of the Book of Genesis. The very process of "subduing the earth," that is to say work, is marked in the course of history and especially in recent centuries by an immense development of technological means. This is an advantageous and positive phenomenon, on condition that the objective dimension of work does not gain the upper hand over the subjective dimension, depriving man of his dignity and inalienable rights or reducing them.

III. CONFLICT BETWEEN LABOR AND CAPITAL IN THE PRESENT PHASE OF HISTORY

11. Dimensions of the Conflict

The sketch of the basic problems of work outlined above draws inspiration from the texts at the beginning of the Bible and in a sense forms the very framework of the Church's teaching, which has remained unchanged throughout the centuries within the context of different historical experiences. However, the experiences preceding and following the publication of the encyclical "Rerum Novarum" form a background that endows that teaching with particular expressiveness and the eloquence of living relevance. In this analysis, work is seen as a great reality with a fundamental influence on the shaping in a human way of the world that the Creator has entrusted to man; it is a reality closely linked with man as the subject of work and with man's rational activity. In the normal course of events this reality fills human life and strongly affects its value and meaning. Even when it is accompanied by toil and effort, work is still something good, and so man develops through love for work. This entirely positive and creative, educational and meritorious character of man's work must be the basis for the judgments and decisions being made today in its regard in spheres that include human rights, as is evidenced by the international declarations on work and the many labor codes prepared either by the competent legislative institutions in the various countries or by organizations devoting their social, or scientific and social, activity to the problems of work. One organization fostering such initiatives on the international level is the International Labor Organization, the oldest specialized agency of the United Nations.

In the following part of these considerations I intend to return in greater detail to those important questions, recalling at least the basic elements of the Church's teaching on the matter. I must however first touch on a very important field of questions in which its teaching has taken shape in this latest period, the one marked and in a sense symbolized by the publication of the encyclical "Rerum Novarum."

Throughout this period, which is by no means yet over, the issue of work has of course been posed on the basis of the great conflict that in the age of and together with industrial development emerged between "capital" and "labor," that is to say between the small but highly influential group of entrepreneurs, owners or holders of the means of production, and the broader multitude of people who lacked these means and who shared in the process of production solely by their labor. The conflict originated in the fact that the workers put their powers at the disposal of the entrepreneurs, and these, following the principle of maximum profit, tried to establish the lowest possible wages for the work done by the employees. In addition there were other elements of exploitation connected with the lack of safety at work and of safeguards regarding the health and living conditions of the workers and their families.

This conflict, interpreted by some as a socio-economic class conflict, found expression in the ideological conflict between liberalism, understood as the ideology of capitalism, and Marxism, understood as the ideology of scientific socialism and communism, which professes to act as the spokesman for the working class and the worldwide proletariat. Thus the real conflict between labor and capital was transformed into a systematic class struggle conducted not only by ideological means, but also and chiefly by political means. We are familiar with the history of this conflict and with the demands of both sides. The Marxist program, based on the philosophy of Marx and Engels, sees in class struggle the only way to eliminate class injustices in society and to eliminate the classes themselves. Putting this program into practice presupposes the collectivization of the means of production so that through the transfer of these means from private hands to the collectivity human labor will be preserved from exploitation.

This is the goal of the struggle carried on by political as well as ideological means. In accordance with the principle of "the dictatorship of the proletariat," the groups that as political parties follow the guidance of Marxist ideology aim by the use of various kinds of influence, including revolutionary pressure, to win a monopoly of power in each society in order to introduce the collectivist system into it by eliminating private ownership of the means of production. According to the principal ideologists and leaders of this broad international movement, the purpose of this program of action is to achieve the social revolution and to introduce socialism and finally the communist system throughout the world.

As we touch on this extremely important field of issues, which constitute not only a theory but a whole fabric of socio-economic, political and international life in our age, we cannot go into the details nor is this necessary for they are known both from the vast literature on the subject and by experience. Instead we must leave the context of these issues and go back to the fundamental issue of human work, which is the main subject of the considerations in this document. It is clear indeed that this issue, which is of such importance for man—it constitutes one of the fundamental dimensions of his earthly existence and of his vocation—can also be explained only by taking into account the full context of the contemporary situation.

12. The Priority of Labor

The structure of the present-day situation is deeply marked by many conflicts caused by man, and the technological means produced by human work play a primary role in it. We should also consider here the prospect of worldwide catastrophe in the case of a

Basic principle: the priority of labor over capital

nuclear war, which would have almost unimaginable possibilities of destruction. In view of this situation we must first of all recall a principle that has always been taught by the Church: the principle of the priority of labor over capital. This principle directly concerns the process of production. In this process labor is always a primary efficient cause, while capital, the whole collection of means of production, remains a mere instrument or instrumental cause. This principle is an evident truth that emerges from the whole of man's historical experience.

When we read in the first chapter of the Bible that man is to subdue the earth, we know that these words refer to all the resources contained in the visible world and placed at man's disposal. However, these resources can serve man only through work. From the beginning there is also linked with work the question of ownership, for the only means that man has for causing the resources hidden in nature to serve himself and others is his work. And to be able through his work to make these resources bear fruit, man takes over ownership of small parts of the various riches of nature: those beneath the ground, those in the sea, on land or in space. He takes over all these things by making them his workbench. He takes them over through work and for work.

The same principle applies in the successive phases of this process, in which the first phase always remains the relationship of man with the resources and riches of nature. The whole of the effort to acquire knowledge with the aim of discovering these riches and specifying the various ways in which they can be used by man and for man teaches us that everything that comes from man throughout the whole process of economic production, whether labor or the whole collection of means of production and the technology connected with these means (meaning the capability to use them in work), presupposes these riches and resources of the visible world, riches and resources that man finds and does not create. In a sense man finds them already prepared, ready for him to discover them and to use them correctly in the productive process. In every phase of the development of his work man comes up against the leading role of the gift made by "nature," that is to say, in the final analysis, by the Creator. At the beginning of man's work is the mystery of creation. This affirmation, already indicated as my starting point, is the guiding thread of this document and will be further developed in the last part of these reflections.

Further consideration of this question should confirm our conviction of the priority of human labor over what in the course of time we have grown accustomed to calling capital. Since the concept of capital includes not only the natural resources placed at man's disposal, but also the whole collection of means by which man appropriates natural resources and transforms them in accordance with his needs (and thus in a sense humanizes them), it must immediately be noted that all these means are the result of the historical heritage of human labor. All the means of production, from the most primitive to the ultra-modern ones—it is man that has gradually developed them: man's experience and intellect. In this way there have appeared not only the simplest instruments for cultivating the earth, but also through adequate progress in science and technology the more modern and complex ones: machines, factories, laboratories and computers. Thus everything that is at the service of work, everything that in the present state of technology constitutes its ever more highly perfected "instrument," is the result of work.

This gigantic and powerful instrument—the whole collection of means of production that in a sense are considered synonymous with "capital"—is the result of work and bears the signs of human labor. At the present stage of technological advance, when man, who is the subject of work, wishes to make use of this collection of modern instruments, the means of production, he must first assimilate cognitively the result of the work of the people who invented those instruments, who planned them, built them and perfected them, and who continue to do so. Capacity for work—that is to say, for sharing efficiently in the modern production process—demands greater and greater preparation and, before all else, proper training. Obviously it remains clear that every human being sharing in the production process, even if he or she is only doing the kind of work for which no special training or qualifications are required, is the real efficient subject in this production process, while the whole collection of instruments, no matter how perfect they may be in themselves, are only a mere instrument subordinate to human labor.

This truth, which is part of the abiding heritage of the Church's teaching, must always be emphasized with reference to the question of the labor system and with regard to the whole socio-economic system. We must emphasize and give prominence to the primacy of man in the production process, the primacy of man over things. Everything contained in the concept of capital in the strict sense is only a collection of things. Man, as the subject of work and independent of the work he does—man alone is a person. This truth has important and decisive consequences.

13. Economism and Materialism

In the light of the above truth we see clearly, first of all, that capital cannot be separated from labor; in no way can labor be opposed to capital or capital to labor, and still less can the actual people behind these concepts be opposed to each other, as will be explained later. A labor system can be right, in the sense of being in conformity with the very essence of the issue and in the sense of being intrinsically true and also morally legitimate, if in its very basis it overcomes the opposition between labor and capital through an effort at being shaped in accordance with the principle put forward above: the principle of the substantial and real priority of labor, of the subjectivity of human labor and its effective participation in the whole production process, independent of the nature of the services provided by the worker.

Opposition between labor and capital does not spring from the structure of the production process or from the structure of the economic process. In general the latter process demonstrates that labor and what we are accustomed to call capital are intermingled; it shows that they are inseparably linked. Working at any workbench, whether a relatively primitive or an ultra-modern one, a man can easily see that through his work he enters into two inheritances: the inheritance of what is given to the whole of humanity in the resources of nature and the inheritance of what others have already developed on the basis of those resources, primarily by developing technology, that is to say, by producing a whole collection of increasingly perfect instruments for work. In working, man also "enters into the labor of others."[21] Guided both by our intelligence and by the faith that draws light from the word of God, we have no difficulty in accepting this image of the sphere and process of man's labor. It is a consistent image, one that is humanistic as well as theological. In it man is the master of the creatures placed at his disposal in the visible world. If some dependence is discovered in the work process, it is dependence on the Giver of all the resources of creation and also on other human beings, those to whose work and initiative we owe the perfected and increased possibilities of our own work. All that we can say of everything in the production process which constitutes a whole collection of "things," the instruments, the capital, is that it conditions man's work; we cannot assert that it constitutes as it were an impersonal "subject" putting man and man's work into a position of dependence.

This consistent image, in which the principle of the primacy of person over things is strictly preserved, was broken up in human thought, sometimes after a long period of incubation in practical living. The break occurred in such a way that labor was separated from capital and set in opposition to it, and capital was set in opposition to labor, as though they were two impersonal forces, two production factors juxtaposed in the same "economistic" perspective. This way of stating the issue contained a fundamental error, what we can call the error of economism, that of considering human labor solely according to its economic purpose. This fundamental error of thought can and must be called an error of materialism, in that economism directly or indirectly includes a conviction of the primacy and superiority of the material, and directly or indirectly places the spiritual and the personal (man's activity, moral values and such matters) in a position of subordination to material reality. This is still not theoretical materialism in the full sense of the term, but it is certainly practical materialism, a materialism judged capable of satisfying man's needs not so much on the grounds of premises derived from materialist theory as on the grounds of a particular way of evaluating things and so on the grounds of a certain hierarchy of goods based on the greater immediate attractiveness of what is material.

The error of thinking in the categories of economism went hand in hand with the formation of a materialist philosophy, as this philosophy developed from the most elementary and common phase (also called common materialism, because it professes to reduce spiritual reality to a superflous phenomenon) to the phase of what is called dialectical materialism. However, within the framework of the present consideration, it seems that economism had a decisive importance for the fundamental issue of human work, in particular for the separation of labor and capital and for setting them up in opposition as two production factors viewed in the above-mentioned economistic perspective; and it seems that economism influenced this non-humanistic way of stating the issue before the materialist philosophical system did. Nevertheless it is obvious that materialism, including its dialectical form, is incapable of providing sufficient and definitive bases for thinking about human work, in order that the primacy of man over the capital instrument, the primacy of the person over things, may find in it adequate and irrefutable confirmation and support. In dialectical materialism too man is not first and foremost the subject of work and efficient cause of the production process, but continues to be understood and treated, in dependence on what is material, as a kind of "resultant" of the economic or production relations prevailing at a given period.

Obviously the antinomy between labor and capital under consideration here—the antinomy in which labor was separated from capital and set up in opposition to it, in a certain sense on the ontic level as if it were just an element like any other in the economic process—did not originate merely in the philosophy and economic theories of the eighteenth century; rather it originated in the whole of the economic and social practice of that time, the time of the birth and rapid development of industrialization, in which what was mainly seen was the possibility of vastly increasing material wealth, means, while the end, that is to say man, who should be served by the means, was ignored. It was this practical error that struck a blow first and foremost against human labor, against the working man, and caused the ethically just social reaction already spoken of above. The same error, which is now part of history and which was connected with the period of primitive capitalism and liberalism, can nevertheless be repeated in other circumstances of time and place if people's thinking starts from the same theoretical or practical premises. The only chance there seems to be for radically overcoming this error is through adequate changes both in theory and in practice, changes in line with the definite conviction of the primacy of the person over things and of human labor over capital as a whole collection of means of production.

14. Work and Ownership

The historical process briefly presented here has certainly gone beyond its initial phase, but it is still taking place and indeed is spreading in the relationships between nations and continents. It needs to be specified further from another point of view. It is obvious that when we speak of opposition between labor and capital, we are not dealing only with abstract concepts or "impersonal forces" operating in economic production. Behind both concepts there are people—living, actual people. On the one side are those who do the work without being the owners of the means of production, and on the other side those who act as entrepreneurs and who own these means or represent the owners. Thus the issue of ownership or property enters from the beginning into the whole of this difficult historical process. The encyclical "Rerum Novarum," which has the social question as its theme, stresses this issue also, recalling and confirming the Church's teaching on ownership, on the right to private property even when it is a question of the means of production. The encyclical "Mater et Magistra" did the same.

The above principle, as it was then stated and as it is still taught by the Church, diverges radically from the program of collectivism as proclaimed by Marxism and put into practice in various countries in the decades following the time of Leo XIII's encyclical. At the same time it differs from the program of capitalism practiced by liberalism and by the political systems inspired by it. In the latter case, the difference consists in the way that the right to ownership or property is understood. Christian tradition has never upheld this right as absolute and untouchable. On the contrary, it has always understood this right within the broader context of the right common to all to use the goods of the whole of creation. The right to private property is subordinated to the right to common use, to the fact that goods are meant for everyone.

Furthermore, in the Church's teaching, ownership has never been understood in a way that could constitute grounds for social conflict in labor. As mentioned above, property is acquired first of all through work in order that it may serve work. This concerns in a special way ownership of the means of production. Isolating these means as a separate property in order to set it up in the form of "capital" in opposition to "labor"—and even to practice exploitation of labor—is contrary to the very nature of these means and their possession. They cannot be possessed against labor, they cannot even be possessed for possession's sake, because the only legitimate title to their possession—whether in the form of private ownership or in the form of public or collective ownership—is that they should serve labor and thus by serving labor that they should make possible the achievement of the first principle of this order, namely the universal destination of goods and the right to common use of them. From this point of view, therefore, in consideration of human labor and of common access to the goods meant for man, one cannot exclude the socialization, in suitable conditions, of certain means of production. In the course of the decades since the publication of the encyclical "Rerum Novarum," the Church's teaching has always recalled all these principles, going back to the arguments formulated in a much older tradition—for example, the well-known arguments of the "Summa Theologiae" of St. Thomas Aquinas.[22]

In the present document, which has human work as its main theme, it is right to confirm all the effort with which the Church's teaching has striven and continues to strive always to ensure the priority of work and thereby man's character as a subject in social life and especially in the dynamic structure of the whole economic process. From this point of view the position of "rigid" capitalism continues to remain unacceptable, namely the position that defends the exclusive right to private ownership of the means of production as an untouchable "dogma" of economic life. The principle of respect for work demands that this right should undergo a constructive revision both in theory and in practice. If it is true that capital, as the whole of the means of production, is at the same time the product of the work of generations, it is equally true that capital is being unceasingly created through the work done with the help of all these means of production, and these means can be seen as a great workbench at which the present generation of workers is working day after day. Obviously we are dealing here with different kinds of work, not only so-called manual labor, but also the many forms of intellectual work, including white-collar work and management.

In the light of the above, the many proposals put forward by experts in Catholic social teaching and by the highest magisterium of

the Church take on special significance:[23] proposals for joint ownership of the means of work, sharing by the workers in the management and/or profits of businesses, so-called shareholding by labor,
etc. Whether these various proposals can or cannot be applied con-
cretely, it is clear that recognition of the proper position of labor and
the worker in the production process demands various adaptations in
the sphere of the right to ownership of the means of production. This
is so not only in view of older situations but also, first and foremost,
in view of the whole of the situation and the problems in the second
half of the present century with regard to the so-called third world
and the various new independent countries that have arisen, especially in Africa but elsewhere as well, in place of the colonial territories
of the past.

Therefore, while the position of "rigid" capitalism must undergo continual revision in order to be reformed from the point of view
of human rights, both human rights in the widest sense and those
linked with man's work, it must be stated that from the same point of
view these many deeply desired reforms cannot be achieved by an a
priori elimination of private ownership of the means of production.
For it must be noted that merely taking these means of production
(capital) out of the hands of their private owners is not enough to
ensure their satisfactory socialization. They cease to be the property
of a certain social group, namely the private owners, and become the
property of organized society, coming under the administration and
direct control of another group of people, namely those who, though
not owning them, from the fact of exercising power in society manage them on the level of the whole national or the local economy.

This group in authority many carry out its task satisfactorily
from the point of view of the priority of labor; but it may also carry it
out badly by claiming for itself a monopoly of the administration and
disposal of the means of production and not refraining even from of-
fending basic human rights. Thus, merely converting the means of
production into state property in the collectivist systems is by no
means equivalent to "socializing" that property. We can speak of socializing only when the subject character of society is ensured, that is
to say, when on the basis of his work each person is fully entitled to
consider himself a part owner of the great workbench at which he is
working with everyone else. A way toward that goal could be found

by associating labor with the ownership of capital, as far as possible, and by producing a wide range of intermediate bodies with economic, social and cultural purposes; they would be bodies enjoying real autonomy with regard to the public powers, pursuing their specific aims in honest collaboration with each other and in subordination to the demands of the common good, and they would be living communities both in form and in substance in the sense that the members of each body would be looked upon and treated as persons and encouraged to take an active part in the life of the body.[24]

15. The "Personalist" Argument

Thus the principle of the priority of labor over capital is a postulate of the order of social morality. It has key importance both in the system built on the principle of the private ownership of the means of production and also in the systems in which private ownership of these means has been limited even in a radical way. Labor is in a sense inseparable from capital; in no way does it accept the antinomy, that is to say, the separation and opposition with regard to the means of production that has weighed upon human life in recent centuries as a result of merely economic premises. When man works, using all the means of production, he also wishes the fruit of this work to be used by himself and others, and he wishes to be able to take part in the very work process as a sharer in responsibility and creativity at the workbench to which he applies himself.

From this spring certain specific rights of workers, corresponding to the obligation of work. They will be discussed later. But here it must be emphasized in general terms that the person who works desires not only due remuneration for his work; he also wishes that within the production process provision be made for him to be able to know that in his work, even on something that is owned in common, he is working "for himself." This awareness is extinguished within him in a system of excessive bureaucratic centralization, which makes the worker feel that he is just a cog in a huge machine moved from above, that he is for more reasons than one a mere production instrument rather than a true subject of work with an initiative of his own. The Church's teaching has always expressed the strong and deep conviction that man's work concerns not only the economy but also, and especially, personal values. The economic system itself and the production process benefit precisely when these personal values are fully respected. In the mind of St. Thomas Aquinas,[25] this is the principal reason in favor of private ownership of the means of production. While we accept that for certain well-founded reasons exceptions can be made to the principle of private ownership—in our own time we even see that the system of "socialized ownership" has been introduced—nevertheless the personalist argument still holds good both on the level of principles and on the practical level. If it is to be rational and fruitful, any socialization of the means of production must take this argument into consideration. Every effort must be made to ensure that in this kind of system also the human person can preserve his awareness of working "for himself." If this is not done, incalculable damage is inevitably done throughout the economic process, not only economic damage but first and foremost damage to man.

IV. RIGHTS OF WORKERS

16. Within the Broad Context of Human Rights

While work, in all its many senses, is an obligation, that is to say a duty, it is also a source of rights on the part of the worker. These rights must be examined in the broad context of human rights as a whole, which are connatural with man and many of which are proclaimed by various international organizations and increasingly guaranteed by the individual states for their citizens. Respect for this broad range of human rights constitutes the fundamental condition for peace in the modern world: peace both within individual countries and societies and in international relations, as the Church's magisterium has several times noted, especially since the encyclical "Pacem in Terris." The human rights that flow from work are part of the broader context of those fundamental rights of the person.

However, within this context they have a specific character corresponding to the specific nature of human work as outlined above. It is in keeping with this character that we must view them. Work is, as has been said, an obligation, that is to say, a duty, on the part of man. This is true in all the many meanings of the word. Man must work both because the Creator has commanded it and because of his own humanity, which requires work in order to be maintained and developed. Man must work out of regard for others, especially his own family, but also for the society he belongs to, the country of which he is a child and the whole human family of which he is a member, since he is the heir to the work of generations and at the same time a sharer in building the future of those who will come after him in the succession of history. All this constitutes the moral obligation of work, understood in its wide sense. When we have to consider the moral rights corresponding to this obligation of every person with regard to work, we must always keep before our eyes the whole vast range of points of reference in which the labor of every working subject is manifested.

For when we speak of the obligation of work and of the rights of the worker that correspond to this obligation, we think in the first place of the relationship between the employer, direct or indirect, and the worker.

The distinction between the direct and the indirect employer is seen to be very important when one considers both the way in which labor is actually organized and the possibility of the formation of just or unjust relationships in the field of labor.

Since the direct employer is the person or institution with whom the worker enters directly into a work contract in accordance with definite conditions, we must understand as the indirect employer many different factors, other than the direct employer, that exercise a determining influence on the shaping both of the work contract and, consequently, of just or unjust relationships in the field of human labor.

17. Direct and Indirect Employer

The concept of indirect employer includes both persons and institutions of various kinds and also collective labor contracts and the principles of conduct which are laid down by these persons and institutions and which determine the whole socio-economic system or are its result. The concept of "indirect employer" thus refers to many different elements. The responsibility of the indirect employer differs

from that of the direct employer—the term itself indicates that the
responsibility is less direct—but it remains a true responsibility. The
indirect employer substantially determines one or other facet of the
labor relationship, thus conditioning the conduct of the direct employer when the latter determines in concrete terms the actual work
contract and labor relations. This is not to absolve the direct employer from his own responsibility, but only to draw attention to the
whole network of influences that condition his conduct. When it is a
question of establishing an ethically correct labor policy, all these influences must be kept in mind. A policy is correct when the objective
rights of the worker are fully respected.

The concept of indirect employer is applicable to every society
and in the first place to the state. For it is the state that must conduct
a just labor policy. However, it is common knowledge that in the
present system of economic relations in the world there are numerous links between individual states, links that find expression, for instance, in the import and export process, that is to say, in the mutual
exchange of economic goods, whether raw materials, semi-manufactured goods or finished industrial products. These links also create
mutual dependence, and as a result it would be difficult to speak in
the case of any state, even the economically most powerful, of complete self-sufficiency or autarky.

Such a system of mutual dependence is in itself normal. However it can easily become an occasion for various forms of exploitation
or injustice and as a result influence the labor policy of individual
states; and finally it can influence the individual worker who is the
proper subject of labor. For instance the highly industrialized countries, and even more the businesses that direct on a large scale the
means of industrial production (the companies referred to as multinational or transnational), fix the highest possible prices for their
products, while trying at the same time to fix the lowest possible
prices for raw materials or semi-manufactured goods. This is one of
the causes of an ever increasing disproportion between national in-
comes. The gap between most of the richest countries and the poorest ones is not diminishing or being stabilized, but is increasing more
and more to the detriment, obviously, of the poor countries. Evident-
ly this must have an effect on local labor policy and on the worker's
situation in the economically disadvantaged societies. Finding him-

self in a system thus conditioned, the direct employer fixes working conditions below the objective requirements of the workers, especially if he himself wishes to obtain the highest possible profits from the business which he runs (or from the businesses which he runs, in the case of a situation of "socialized" ownership of the means of production).

It is easy to see that this framework of forms of dependence linked with the concept of the indirect employer is enormously extensive and complicated. It is determined, in a sense, by all the elements that are decisive for economic life within a given society and state, but also by much wider links and forms of dependence. The attainment of the worker's rights cannot however be doomed to be merely a result of economic systems which on a larger or smaller scale are guided chiefly by the criterion of maximum profit. On the contrary, it is respect for the objective rights of the worker—every kind of worker: manual or intellectual, industrial or agricultural, etc.—that must constitute the adequate and fundamental criterion for shaping the whole economy, both on the level of the individual society and state and within the whole of the world economic policy and of the systems of international relationships that derive from it.

Influence in this direction should be exercised by all the international organizations whose concern it is, beginning with the United Nations. It appears that the International Labor Organization and the Food and Agriculture Organization of the United Nations and other bodies too have fresh contributions to offer on this point in particular. Within the individual states there are ministries or public departments and also various social institutions set up for this purpose. All of this effectively indicates the importance of the indirect employer—as has been said above—in achieving full respect for the worker's rights, since the rights of the human person are the key element in the whole of the social moral order.

18. The Employment Issue

When we consider the rights of workers in relation to the "indirect employer," that is to say, all the agents at the national and international level that are responsible for the whole orientation of labor policy, we must first direct our attention to a fundamental issue: the question of finding work or, in other words, the issue of suitable employment for all who are capable of it. The opposite of a just and right situation in this field is unemployment, that is to say, the lack of work for those who are capable of it. It can be a question of general unemployment or of unemployment in certain sectors of work. The role of the agents included under the title of indirect employer is to act against unemployment, which in all cases is an evil and which, when it reaches a certain level, can become a real social disaster. It is particularly painful when it especially affects young people, who after appropriate cultural, technical and professional preparation fail to find work and see their sincere wish to work and their readiness to take on their own responsibility for the economic and social development of the community sadly frustrated. The obligation to provide unemployment benefits, that is to say, the duty to make suitable grants indispensable for the subsistence of unemployed workers and their families, is a duty springing from the fundamental principle of the moral order in this sphere, namely the principle of the common use of goods or, to put it in another and still simpler way, the right to life and subsistence.

In order to meet the danger of unemployment and to ensure employment for all, the agents defined here as "indirect employer" must make provision for overall planning with regard to the different kinds of work by which not only the economic life, but also the cultural life of a given society is shaped; they must also give attention to organizing that work in a correct and rational way. In the final analysis this overall concern weighs on the shoulders of the state, but it cannot mean one-sided centralization by the public authorities. Instead, what is in question is a just and rational coordination, within the framework of which the initiative of individuals, free groups and local work centers and complexes must be safeguarded, keeping in mind what has been said above with regard to the subject character of human labor.

The fact of the mutual dependence of societies and states and the need to collaborate in various areas mean that, while preserving the sovereign rights of each society and state in the field of planning and organizing labor in its own society, action in this important area must also be taken in the dimension of international collaboration by means of the necessary treaties and agreements. Here too the criterion for these pacts and agreements must more and more be the criterion of human work considered as a fundamental right of all human beings, work which gives similar rights to all those who work in such a way that the living standard of the workers in the different societies will less and less show those disturbing differences which are unjust and are apt to provoke even violent reactions. The international organizations have an enormous part to play in this area. They must let themselves be guided by an exact diagnosis of the complex situations and of the influence exercised by natural, historical, civil and other such circumstances. They must also be more highly operative with regard to plans for action jointly decided on, that is to say, they must be more effective in carrying them out.

In this direction, it is possible to actuate a plan for universal and proportionate progress by all in accordance with the guidelines of Paul VI's encyclical "Populorum Progressio." It must be stressed that the constitutive element in this progress and also the most adequate way to verify it in a spirit of justice and peace, which the Church proclaims and for which it does not cease to pray to the Father of all individuals and of all peoples, is the continual reappraisal of man's work, both in the aspect of its objective finality and in the aspect of the dignity of the subject of all work, that is to say, man. The progress in question must be made through man and for man and it must produce its fruit in man. A test of this progress will be the increasingly mature recognition of the purpose of work and increasingly universal respect for the rights inherent in work in conformity with the dignity of man, the subject of work.

Rational planning and the proper organization of human labor in keeping with individual societies and states should also facilitate the discovery of the right proportions between the different kinds of employment: work on the land, in industry, in the various services, white-collar work and scientific or artistic work, in accordance with the capacities of individuals and for the common good of each society and of the whole of mankind. The organization of human life in accordance with the many possibilities of labor should be matched by a suitable system of instruction and education aimed first of all at developing mature human beings, but also aimed at preparing people specifically for assuming to good advantage an appropriate place in the vast and socially differentiated world of work.

As we view the whole human family throughout the world, we cannot fail to be struck by a disconcerting fact of immense proportions: the fact that while conspicuous natural resources remain unused there are huge numbers of people who are unemployed or underemployed and countless multitudes of people suffering from hunger. This is a fact that without any doubt demonstrates that both within the individual political communities and in their relationships on the continental and world levels there is something wrong with the organization of work and employment, precisely at the most critical and socially most important points.

19. Wages and Other Social Benefits

After outlining the important role that concern for providing employment for all workers plays in safeguarding respect for the inalienable rights of man in view of his work, it is worthwhile taking a closer look at these rights, which in the final analysis are formed within the relationship between worker and direct employer. All that has been said above on the subject of the indirect employer is aimed at defining these relationships more exactly, by showing the many forms of conditioning within which these relationships are indirectly formed. This consideration does not however have a purely descriptive purpose; it is not a brief treatise on economics or politics. It is a matter of highlighting the deonotological and moral aspect. The key problem of social ethics in this case is that of just remuneration for work done. In the context of the present there is no more important way for securing a just relationship between the worker and the employer than that constituted by remuneration for work. Whether the work is done in a system of private ownership of the means of production or in a system where ownership has undergone a certain "socialization," the relationship between the employer (first and foremost the direct employer) and the worker is resolved on the basis of the wage, that is, through just remuneration for the work done.

It should also be noted that the justice of a socio-economic system and, in each case, its just functioning deserve in the final analysis to be evaluated by the way in which man's work is properly remunerated in the system. Here we return once more to the first principle of the whole ethical and social order, namely the principle of the common use of goods. In every system, regardless of the fundamental relationships within it between capital and labor, wages, that is to say remuneration for work, are still a practical means whereby the vast majority of people can have access to those goods which are intended for common use: both the goods of nature and manufactured goods. Both kinds of goods become accessible to the worker through the wage which he receives as remuneration for his work. Hence in every case a just wage is the concrete means of verifying the justice of the whole socio-economic system and, in any case, of checking that it is functioning justly. It is not the only means of checking, but it is a particularly important one and in a sense the key means.

This means of checking concerns above all the family. Just remuneration for the work of an adult who is responsible for a family means remuneration which will suffice for establishing and properly maintaining a family and for providing security for its future. Such remuneration can be given either through what is called a family wage—that is, a single salary given to the head of the family for his work, sufficient for the needs of the family without the other spouse having to take up gainful employment outside the home—or through other social measures such as family allowances or grants to mothers devoting themselves exclusively to their families. These grants should correspond to the actual needs, that is, to the number of dependents for as long as they are not in a position to assume proper responsibility for their own lives.

Experience confirms that there must be a social re-evaluation of the mother's role, of the toil connected with it and of the need that children have for care, love and affection in order that they may develop into responsible, morally and religiously mature and psychologically stable persons. It will redound to the credit of society to make it possible for a mother—without inhibiting her freedom, without psychological or practical discrimination, and without penalizing her as compared with other women—to devote herself to taking care of her children and educating them in accordance with their needs, which vary with age. Having to abandon these tasks in order to take up paid work outside the home is wrong from the point of view of the good of society and of the family when it contradicts or hinders these primary goals of the mission of a mother.[26]

In this context it should be emphasized that on a more general level the whole labor process must be organized and adapted in such a way as to respect the requirements of the person and his or her forms of life, above all life in the home, taking into account the individual's age and sex. It is a fact that in many societies women work in nearly every sector of life. But it is fitting that they should be able to fulfill their tasks in accordance with their own nature, without being discriminated against and without being excluded from jobs for which they are capable, but also without lack of respect for their family aspirations and for their specific role in contributing, together with men, to the good of society. The true advancement of women requires that labor should be structured in such a way that women do not have to pay for their advancement by abandoning what is specific to them and at the expense of the family, in which women as mothers have an irreplaceable role.

Besides wages, various social benefits intended to ensure the life and health of workers and their families play a part here. The expenses involved in health care, especially in the case of accidents at work, demand that medical assistance should be easily available for workers and that as far as possible it should be cheap or even free of charge. Another sector regarding benefits is the sector associated with the right to rest. In the first place this involves a regular weekly rest comprising at least Sunday and also a longer period of rest, namely the holiday or vacation taken once a year or possibly in several shorter periods during the year. A third sector concerns the right to a pension and to insurance for old age and in case of accidents at work. Within the sphere of these principal rights there develops a whole system of particular rights which, together with remuneration for work, determine the correct relationship between worker and employer. Among these rights there should never be overlooked the right to a working environment and to manufacturing processes which are not harmful to the workers' physical health or to their moral integrity.

20. Importance of Unions

All these rights, together with the need for the workers themselves to secure them, give rise to yet another right: the right of association, that is, to form associations for the purpose of defending the vital interests of those employed in the various professions. These associations are called labor or trade unions. The vital interests of the workers are to a certain extent common for all of them; at the same time, however, each type of work, each profession, has its own specific character which should find a particular reflection in these organizations.

In a sense, unions go back to the medieval guilds of artisans, insofar as those organizations brought together people belonging to the same craft and thus on the basis of their work. However unions differ from the guilds on this essential point: the modern unions grew up from the struggle of the workers—in general but especially the industrial workers—to protect their just rights vis-à-vis the entrepreneurs and the owners of the means of production. Their task is to defend the existential interests of workers in all sectors in which their rights are concerned. The experience of history teaches that organizations of this type are an indispensable element of social life, especially in modern industrialized societies. Obviously this does not mean that only industrial workers can set up associations of this type. Representatives of every profession can use them to ensure their own rights. Thus there are unions of agricultural workers and of white-collar workers; there are also employers' associations. All, as has been said above, are further divided into groups or subgroups according to particular professional specializations.

Catholic social teaching does not hold that unions are no more than a reflection of the "class" structure of society and that they are a mouthpiece for a class struggle which inevitably governs social life. They are indeed a mouthpiece for the struggle for social justice, for the just rights of working people in accordance with their individual professions. However, this struggle should be seen as a normal endeavor "for" the just good—in the present case, for the good which corresponds to the needs and merits of working people associated by profession—but it is not a struggle "against" others. Even if in controversial questions the struggle takes on a character of opposition toward others, this is because it aims at the good of social justice, not for the sake of "struggle" or in order to eliminate the opponent. It is characteristic of work that it first and foremost unites people. In this consists its social power: the power to build a community. In the final analysis, both those who work and those who manage the means of production or who own them must in some way be united in this community. In the light of this fundamental structure of all work—in the light of the fact that, in the final analysis, labor and capital are indispensable components of the process of production in any social system—it is clear that even if it is because of their work needs that people unite to secure their rights, their union remains a constructive factor of social order and solidarity, and it is impossible to ignore it.

Just efforts to secure the rights of workers who are united by the same profession should always take into account the limitations imposed by the general economic situation of the country. Union demands cannot be turned into a kind of group of class "egosim," although they can and should also aim at correcting—with a view to the common good of the whole of society—everything defective in the system of ownership of the means of production or in the way these are managed. Social and socio-economic life is certainly like a system of "connected vessels," and every social activity directed toward safeguarding the rights of particular groups should adapt itself to this system.

In this sense, union activity undoubtedly enters the field of politics, understood as prudent concern for the common good. However, the role of unions is not to "play politics" in the sense that the expression is commonly understood today. Unions do not have the character of political parties struggling for power; they should not be subjected to the decision of political parties or have too close links with them. In fact, in such a situation they easily lose contact with their specific role, which is to secure the just rights of workers within the framework of the common good of the whole of society; instead they become an instrument used for other purposes.

Speaking of the protection of the just rights of workers according to their individual professions, we must of course always keep in mind that which determines the subjective character of work in each profession, but at the same time, indeed before all else, we must keep in mind that which conditions the specific dignity of the subject of the work. The activity of union organizations opens up many possibilities in this respect, including their efforts to instruct and educate the workers and to foster their self-education. Praise is due to the work of the schools, what are known as workers' or people's universities and the training programs and courses which have developed and are still developing this field of activity. It is always to be hoped that, thanks to the work of their unions, workers will not only have more, but above all be more: in other words that they will realize their humanity more fully in every respect.

One method used by unions in pursuing the just rights of their members is the strike or work stoppage, as a kind of ultimatum to the competent bodies, especially the employers. This method is recognized by Catholic social teaching as legitimate in the proper conditions and within just limits.

In this connection workers should be assured the right to strike, without being subjected to personal penal sanctions for taking part in a strike. While admitting that it is a legitimate means, we must at the same time emphasize that a strike remains, in a sense, an extreme means. It must not be abused; it must not be abused especially for "political" purposes.

Furthermore, it must never be forgotten that, when essential community services are in question, they must in every case be ensured, if necessary by means of appropriate legislation. Abuse of the strike weapon can lead to the paralysis of the whole of socio-economic life, and this is contrary to the requirements of the common good of society, which also corresponds to the properly understood nature of work itself.

21. Dignity of Agricultural Work

All that has been said thus far on the dignity of work, on the objective and subjective dimension of human work, can be directly applied to the question of agricultural work and to the situation of the person who cultivates the earth by toiling in the fields.

This is a vast sector of work on our planet, a sector not restricted to one or other continent, nor limited to the societies which have already attained a cetain level of development and progress. The world of agriculture, which provides society with the goods it needs for its daily sustenance, is of fundamental importance.

The conditions of the rural population and of agricultural work vary from place to place, and the social position of agricultural workers differs from country to country. This depends not only on the level of development of agricultural technology but also, and perhaps more, on the recognition of the just rights of agricultural workers and, finally, on the level of awareness regarding the social ethics of work.

Agricultural work involves considerable difficulties, including unremitting and sometimes exhausting physical effort and a lack of appreciation on the part of society, to the point of making agricultural people feel that they are social outcasts and of speeding up the phenomenon of their mass exodus from the countryside to the cities and unfortunately to still more dehumanizing living conditions. Added to this are the lack of adequate professional training and of proper equipment, the spread of a certain individualism, and also objectively unjust situations. In certain developing countries, millions of people are forced to cultivate the land belonging to others and are exploited by the big landowners, without any hope of ever being able to gain possession of even a small piece of land of their own. There is a lack of forms of legal protection for the agricultural workers themselves and for their families in case of old age, sickness or unemployment. Long days of hard physical work are paid miserably. Land which could be cultivated is left abandoned by the owners. Legal titles to possession of a small portion of land that someone has personally cultivated for years are disregarded or left defenseless against the "land hunger" of more powerful individuals or groups. But even in the economically developed countries, where scientific research, technological achievements and state policy have brought agriculture to a very advanced level, the right to work can be infringed when the farmworkers are denied the possibility of sharing in decisions concerning their services, or when they are denied the right to free association with a view to their just advancement socially, culturally and economically.

In many situations radical and urgent changes are therefore needed in order to restore to agriculture—and to rural people—their just value as the basis for a healthy economy, within the social community's development as a whole. Thus it is necessary to proclaim and promote the dignity of work, of all work but especially of agricultural work, in which man so eloquently "subdues" the earth he has received as a gift from God and affirms his "dominion" in the visible world.

22. The Disabled Person and Work

Recently, national communities and international organizations have turned their attention to another question connected with work, one full of implications: the question of disabled people. They too are fully human subjects with corresponding innate, sacred and inviolable rights, and, in spite of the limitations and sufferings affecting their bodies and faculties, they point up more clearly the dignity and greatness of man. Since disabled people are subjects with all their rights, they should be helped to participate in the life of society in all its aspects and at all the levels accessible to their capacities. The disabled person is one of us and participates fully in the same humanity that we possess. It would be radically unworthy of man, and a denial of our common humanity, to admit to the life of the community, and thus admit to work, only those who are fully functional. To do so would be to practice a serious form of discrimination, that of the strong and healthy against the weak and sick. Work in the objective sense should be subordinated, in this circumstance too, to the dignity of man, to the subject of work and not to economic advantage.

The various bodies involved in the world of labor, both the direct and the indirect employer, should therefore, by means of effective and appropriate measures, foster the right of disabled people to professional training and work, so that they can be given a productive activity suited to them. Many practical problems arise at this point, as well as legal and economic ones; but the community, that is to say, the public authorities, associations and intermediate groups, business enterprises and the disabled themselves, should pool their ideas and resources so as to attain this goal that must not be shirked: that disabled people may be offered work according to their capabilities, for this is demanded by their dignity as persons and as subjects of work. Each community will be able to set up suitable structures for finding or creating jobs for such people both in the usual public or private enterprises, by offering them ordinary or suitably adapted jobs, and in what are called "protected" enterprises and surroundings.

Careful attention must be devoted to the physical and psychological working conditions of disabled pepole—as for all workers—to their just remuneration, to the possibility of their promotion, and to the elimination of various obstacles. Without hiding the fact that this is a complex and difficult task, it is to be hoped that a correct concept of labor in the subjective sense will produce a situation which will make it possible for disabled people to feel that they are not cut off from the working world or dependent upon society, but that they are full-scale subjects of work, useful, respected for their human dignity and called to contribute to the progress and welfare of their families and of the community according to their particular capacities.

23. Work and the Emigration Question

Finally, we must say at least a few words on the subject of emigration in search of work. This is an age-old phenomenon which nevertheless continues to be repeated and is still today very widespread as a result of the complexities of modern life.

Man has the right to leave his native land for various motives—and also the right to return—in order to seek better conditions of life in another country. This fact is certainly not without difficulties of various kinds. Above all it generally constitutes a loss for the country which is left behind. It is the departure of a person who is also a member of a great community united by history, tradition and culture; and that person must begin life in the midst of another society united by a different culture and very often by a different language. In this case, it is the loss of a subject of work, whose efforts of mind and body could contribute to the common good of his own country, but these efforts, this contribution, are instead offered to another society which in a sense has less right to them than the person's country of origin.

Nevertheless, even if emigration is in some aspects an evil, in certain circumstances it is, as the phrase goes, a necessary evil. Everything should be done—and certainly much is being done to this end—to prevent this material evil from causing greater moral harm; indeed every possible effort should be made to ensure that it may bring benefit to the emigrant's personal, family and social life, both for the country to which he goes and the country which he leaves. In this area much depends on just legislation, in particular with regard to the rights of workers. It is obvious that the question of just legislation enters into the context of the present considerations, especially from the point of view of these rights.

The most important thing is that the person working away from his native land, whether as a permanent emigrant or as a seasonal worker, should not be placed at a disadvantage in comparison with the other workers in that society in the matter of working rights. Emigration in search of work must in no way become an opportunity for financial or social exploitation. As regards the work relationship, the same criteria should be applied to immigrant workers as to all other workers in the society concerned. The value of work should be measured by the same standard and not according to the difference in nationality, religion or race. For even greater reason the situation of constraint in which the emigrant may find himself should not be exploited. All these circumstances should categorically give way, after special qualifications have of course been taken into consideration, to the fundamental value of work, which is bound up with the dignity of the human person. Once more the fundamental principle must be repeated: the hierarchy of values and the profound meaning of work itself require that capital should be at the service of labor and not labor at the service of capital.

V. ELEMENTS FOR A SPIRITUALITY OF WORK

24. A Particular Task for the Church

It is right to devote the last part of these reflections about human work, on the occasion of the ninetieth anniversary of the encyclical "Rerum Novarum," to the spirituality of work in the Christian sense. Since work in its subjective aspect is always a personal action, an "actus personae," it follows that the whole person, body and spirit, participates in it, whether it is manual or intellectual work. It is also to the whole person that the word of the living God is directed, the evangelical message of salvation, in which we find many points which concern human work and which throw particular light on it.

These points need to be properly assimilated. An inner effort on the part of the human spirit, guided by faith, hope and charity, is needed in order that through these points the work of the individual human being may be given the meaning which it has in the eyes of God and by means of which work enters into the salvation process on a par with the other ordinary yet particularly important components of its texture.

The Church considers it to be its duty to speak out on work from the viewpoint of its human value and of the moral order to which it belongs, and it sees this as one of its important tasks within the service that it renders to the evangelical message as a whole.

At the same time the Church sees it as its particular duty to form a spirituality of work which will help all people to come closer, through work, to God, the Creator and Redeemer, to participate in his salvific plan for man and the world and to deepen their friendship with Christ in their lives by accepting, through faith, a living participation in his threefold mission as priest, prophet and king, as the Second Vatican Council so eloquently teaches.

25. Work as a Sharing in the Activity of the Creator

As the Second Vatican Council says, "throughout the course of the centuries, men have labored to better the circumstances of their lives through a monumental amount of individual and collective effort. To believers, this point is settled. Considered in itself, such human activity accords with God's will. For man, created to God's image, received a mandate to subject to himself the earth and all that it contains, and to govern the world with justice and holiness—a mandate to relate himself and the totality of things to him who was to be acknowledged as the Lord and Creator of all. Thus, by the subjection of all things to man, the name of God would be wonderful in all the earth."[27]

The word of God's revelation is profoundly marked by the fundamental truth that man, created in the image of God, shares by his work in the activity of the Creator and that, within the limits of his own human capabilities, man in a sense continues to develop that activity, and perfects it as he advances further and further in the discovery of the resources and values contained in the whole of creation. We find this truth at the very beginning of Sacred Scripture, in the Book of Genesis, where the creation activity itself is presented in the form of "work" done by God during "six days,"[28] "resting" on the seventh day.[29] Besides, the last book of Sacred Scripture echoes the same respect for what God has done through his creative "work" when it proclaims: "Great and wonderful are your deeds, O Lord God the Almighty."[30] This is similar to the Book of Genesis, which concludes the description of each day of creation with the statement: "And God saw that it was good."[31]

This description of creation, which we find in the very first chapter of the Book of Genesis, is also in a sense the first "gospel of work," for it shows what the dignity of work consists of. It teaches that man ought to imitate God, his Creator, in working, because man alone has the unique characteristic of likeness to God. Man ought to imitate God both in working and also in resting, since God himself wished to present his own creative activity under the form of work and rest.

This activity by God in the world always continues, as the words of Christ attest: "My Father is working still. . . ."[32] He works with creative power by sustaining in existence the world that he called into being from nothing, and he works with salvific power in the hearts of those whom from the beginning he has destined for "rest"[33] in union with himself in his "Father's house."[34]

Therefore man's work too not only requires a rest every "seventh day,"[35] but also cannot consist in the mere exercise of human strength in external action; it must leave room for man to prepare himself, by becoming more and more what in the will of God he ought to be, for the "rest" that the Lord reserves for his servants and friends.[36]

Awareness that man's work is a participation in God's activity ought to permeate, as the Council teaches, even "the most ordinary everyday activities. For, while providing the substance of life for themselves and their families, men and women are performing their activities in a way which appropriately benefits society. They can justly consider that by their labor they are unfolding the Creator's work, consulting the advantages of their brothers and sisters, and contributing by their personal industry to the realization in history of the divine plan."[37]

This Christian spirituality of work should be a heritage shared by all. Especially in the modern age, the spirituality of work should show the maturity called for by the tensions and restlessness of mind and heart.

"Far from thinking that works produced by man's own talent and energy are in opposition to God's power, and that the rational creature exists as a kind of rival to the Creator, Christians are convinced that the triumphs of the human race are a sign of God's greatness and the flowering of his own mysterious design. For the greater man's power becomes, the farther his individual and community responsibility extends. . . . People are not deterred by the Christian message from building up the world, or impelled to neglect the welfare of their fellows. They are, rather, more stringently bound to do these very things."[38]

The knowledge that by means of work man shares in the work of creation constitutes the most profound motive for undertaking it in various sectors. "The faithful, therefore," we read in the Constitution "Lumen Gentium," "must learn the deepest meaning and the value of all creation, and its orientation to the praise of God. Even by their secular activity they must assist one another to live holier lives. In this way the world will be permeated by the spirit of Christ and more effectively achieve its purpose in justice, charity and peace. . . . Therefore, by their competence in secular fields and by their personal activity, elevated from within by the grace of Christ, let them work vigorously so that by human labor, technical skill, and civil culture, created goods may be perfected according to the design of the Creator and the light of his word."[39]

26. Christ: The Man of Work

The truth that by means of work man participates in the activity of God himself, his Creator, was given particular prominence by Jesus Christ—the Jesus at whom many of his first listeners in Nazareth "were astonished, saying, "Where did this man get all this? What is the wisdom given to him? . . . Is not this the carpenter'?"[40]

For Jesus not only proclaimed but first and foremost fulfilled by his deeds the "Gospel," the word of eternal wisdom, that had been entrusted to him. Therefore, this was also "the gospel of work," because he who proclaimed it was himself a man of work, a craftsman like Joseph of Nazareth.[41] And if we do not find in his words a special command to work—but rather on one occasion a prohibition against too much anxiety about work and life[42]—at the same time the eloquence of the life of Christ is unequivocal. He belongs to the "working world," he has appreciation and respect for human work. It can indeed be said that he looks with love upon human work and the different forms that it takes, seeing in each one of these forms a particular facet of man's likeness with God, the Creator and Father. Is it not he who says: "My Father is the vinedresser"[43] and in various ways puts into his teaching the fundamental truth about work which is already expressed in the whole tradition of the Old Testament, beginning with the Book of Genesis?

The books of the Old Testament contain main references to human work and to the individual professions exercised by man: for example, the doctor,[44] the pharmacist,[45] the craftsman or artist,[46] the blacksmith[47]—we could apply these words to today's foundry-workers—the potter,[48] the farmer,[49] the scholar,[50] the sailor,[51] the builder,[52] the musician,[53] the shepherd,[54] and the fisherman.[55]

The words of praise for the work of women are well known.[56] In his parables on the kingdom of God, Jesus Christ constantly refers to human work: that of the shepherd,[57] the farmer,[58] the doctor,[59] the sower,[60] the householder,[61] the servant,[62] the steward,[63] the fisherman,[64] the merchant,[65] and the laborer.[66] He also speaks of the various forms of women's work.[67] He compares the apostolate to the manual work of harvesters[68] or fishermen.[69] He refers to the work of scholars too.[70]

This teaching of Christ on work, based on the example of his life during his years in Nazareth, finds a particularly lively echo in the teaching of the apostle Paul. Paul boasts of working at his trade (he was probably a tentmaker),[71] and thanks to that work he was able even as an apostle to earn his own bread.[72] "With toil and labor we worked night and day, that we might not burden any of you."[73] Hence his instructions, in the form of exhortation and command, on the subject of work: "Now such persons we command and exhort in the Lord Jesus Christ to do their work in quietness and to earn their own living," he writes to the Thessalonians.[74] In fact, noting that some "are living in idleness ... not doing any work,"[75] the apostle does not hesitate to say in the same context: "If anyone will not work, let him not eat."[76] In another passage he encourages his readers: "Whatever your task, work heartily, as serving the Lord and not men, knowing that from the Lord you will receive the inheritance as your reward."[77]

The teachings of the apostle of the Gentiles obviously have key importance for the morality and spirituality of human work. They are an important complement to the great though discreet gospel of work that we find in the life and parables of Christ, in what Jesus "did and taught."[78]

On the basis of these illuminations emanating from the source himself, the Church has always proclaimed what we find expressed in modern terms in the teaching of the Second Vatican Council: "Just as human activity proceeds from man, so it is ordered toward man. For when a man works he not only alters things and society, he develops himself as well. He learns much, he cultivates his resources, he goes outside of himself and beyond himself. Rightly understood, this kind of growth is of greater value than any external riches which can be garnered. ... Hence, the norm of human activity is this: that in accord with the divine plan and will, it should harmonize with the genuine good of the human race, and allow people as individuals and as members of society to pursue their total vocation and fulfill it."[79]

Such a vision of the values of human work, or in other words such a spirituality of work, fully explains what we read in the same section of the Council's Pastoral Constitution with regard to the right meaning of progress: "A person is more precious for what he is than for what he has. Similarly, all that people do to obtain greater justice, wider brotherhood, and a more humane ordering of social relationships has greater worth than technical advances. For these advances can supply the material for human progress, but of themselves alone they can never actually bring it about."[80]

This teaching on the question of progress and development—a subject that dominates present-day thought—can be understood only as the fruit of a tested spirituality of human work; and it is only on the basis of such a spirituality that it can be realized and put into practice. This is the teaching, and also the program, that has its roots in "the gospel of work."

27. Human Work in the Light of the
Cross and the Resurrection of Christ

There is yet another aspect of human work, an essential dimension of it, that is profoundly imbued with the spirituality based on the Gospel. All work, whether manual or intellectual, is inevitably linked with toil. The Book of Genesis expresses it in a truly penetrating manner: the original blessing of work contained in the very mystery of creation and connected with man's elevation as the image of God is contrasted with the curse that sin brought with it: "Cursed is the ground because of you; in toil you shall eat of it all the days of your life."[81] This toil connected with work marks the way of human life on earth and constitutes an announcement of death: "In the sweat of your face you shall eat bread till you return to the ground, for out of it you were taken."[82] Almost as an echo of these words, the author of one of the wisdom books says: "Then I considered all that my hands had done and the toil I had spent in doing it."[83] There is no one on earth who could not apply these words to himself.

In a sense, the final word of the Gospel on this matter as on others is found in the paschal mystery of Jesus Christ. It is here that we must seek an answer to these problems so important for the spirituality of human work. The paschal mystery contains the cross of Christ and his obedience unto death, which the apostle contrasts with the disobedience which from the beginning has burdened man's history on earth.[84] It also contains the elevation of Christ, who by means of death on a cross returns to his disciples in the resurrection with the power of the Holy Spirit.

Sweat and toil, which work necessarily involves in the present condition of the human race, present the Christian and everyone who is called to follow Christ with the possibility of sharing lovingly in the work that Christ came to do.[85] This work of salvation came about through suffering and death on a cross. By enduring the toil of work in union with Christ crucified for us, man in a way collaborates with the Son of God for the redemption of humanity. He shows himself a true disciple of Christ by carrying the cross in his turn every day[86] in the activity that he is called upon to perform.

Christ, "undergoing death itself for all of us sinners, taught us by example that we too must shoulder that cross which the world and the flesh inflict upon those who pursue peace and justice;" but also, at the same time, "appointed Lord by his resurrection and given all authority in heaven and on earth, Christ is now at work in people's hearts through the power of his Spirit. . . . He animates, purifies and strengthens those noble longings too by which the human family strives to make its life more human and to render the whole earth submissive to this goal."[87]

The Christian finds in human work a small part of the cross of Christ and accepts it in the same spirit of redemption in which Christ accpeted his cross for us. In work, thanks to the light that penetrates us from the resurrection of Christ, we always find a glimmer of new life, of the new good, as if it were an announcement of "the new heavens and the new earth"[88] in which man and the world participate precisely through the toil that goes with work: through toil—and never without it. On the one hand this confirms the indispensability of the cross in the spirituality of human work; on the other hand the cross which this toil constitutes reveals a new good springing from work itself, from work understood in depth and in all its aspects and never apart from work.

Is this new good—the fruit of human work—already a small part of that "new earth" where justice dwells?[89] If it is true that the many forms of toil that go with man's work are a small part of the cross of Christ, what is the relationship of this new good to the resurrection of Christ? The Council seeks to reply to this question also, drawing light from the very sources of the revealed word: "Therefore, while we are warned that it profits a man nothing if he gains the whole world and loses himself (cf. Lk 9:25), the expectation of a new earth must not weaken but rather stimulate our concern for cultivating this one. For here grows the body of a new human family, a body which even now is able to give some kind of foreshadowing of the new age. Earthly progress must be carefully distinguished from the growth of Christ's kingdom. Nevertheless, to the extent that the former can contribute to the better ordering of human society, it is of vital concern to the kingdom of God."[90]

In these present reflections devoted to human work we have tried to emphasize everything that seemed essential to it, since it is through man's labor that not only "the fruits of our activity" but also "human dignity, brotherhood and freedom" must increase on earth.[91] Let the Christian who listens to the word of the living God, uniting work with prayer, know the place that his work has not only in earthly progress but also in the development of the kingdom of God, to which we are all called through the power of the Holy Spirit and through the word of the Gospel.

In concluding these reflections, I gladly impart the apostolic blessing to all of you, venerable brothers and beloved sons and daughters.

I prepared this document for publication on last May 15, on the ninetieth anniversary of the encyclical "Rerum Novarum," but it is only after my stay in the hospital that I have been able to revise it definitively.

Given at Castelgandolfo, on the 14th day of September, the feast of the triumph of the cross, in the year 1981, the third of the pontificate.

NOTES

1. Cf. Ps 127 (128):2; cf. also Gen 3:17–19; Prov 10:22; Ex 1:8–14; Jer 22:13.

2. Cf. Gen 1:26.

3. Cf. Gen 1:28.

4. Encyclical "Redemptor Hominis," 14: AAS 71 (1979), p. 284.

5. Cf. Ps 127(128):2.

6. Gen 3:19.

7. Cf. Mt 13:52.

8. Second Vatican Ecumenical Council, Pastoral Constitution on the Church in the Modern World "Gaudium et Spes," 38: AAS 58 (1966), p. 1055.

9. Gen 1:27.

10. Gen 1:28.

11. Cf. Heb 2:17; Phil 2:5–8.

12. Cf. Pope Pius XI, Encyclical "Quadragesimo Anno": AAS 23 (1931), p. 221.

13. Dt 24:15; Jas 5:4; and also Gen 4:10.

14. Cf. Gen 1:28.

15. Cf. Gen 1:26–27.

16. Gen 3:19.

17. Heb 6:8; cf. Gen 3:18.

18. Cf. "Summa Th.," I–II, q. 40, a. 1. c.; I–II, q. 34, a. 2, ad 1.

19. Cf. "Summa Th.," I–II, q. 40, a. 1, c.; I–II, q. 34, a. 2, ad 1.

20. Cf. Pope Pius XI, Encyclical "Quadragesimo Anno": AAS 23 (1931), pp. 221–222.

21. Cf. Jn 4:38.

22. On the right to property see "Summa Th.," II–II, q. 66, arts. 2 and 6; "De Regimine Principum," book 1, chapters 15 and 17. On the social function of property see "Summa Th.," II–II, q. 134, art. 1, ad 3.

23. Cf. Pope Pius XI, Encyclical "Quadragesimo Anno": AAS 23 (1931), p. 199; Second Vatican Council, Pastoral Constitution on the Church in the Modern World, "Gaudium et Spes," 68: AAS 58 (1966), pp. 1089–1090.

24. Cf. Pope John XXIII, Encyclical "Mater et Magistra": AAS 53 (1961), p. 419.

25. Cf. "Summa Th.," II–II, q. 65, a. 2.

26. Second Vatican Ecumenical Council, Pastoral Constitution on the Church in the Modern World "Gaudium et Spes," 67: AAS 58 (1966), p. 1089.

27. Second Vatican Ecumenical Council, Pastoral Constitution on the Church in the Modern World, "Gaudium et Spes," 34: AAS 58 (1966), pp. 1053–1053.

28. Cf. Gen 2:2; Ex 20:8, 11; Dt 5:12–14.

29. Cf. Gen 2:3.

30. Rev 15:3.

31. Gen 1:4, 10, 12, 18, 21, 25, 31.

32. Jn 5:17.

33. Cf. Heb 4:1, 9–10.

34. Jn 14:2.

35. Cf. Dt 5:12–14; Ex 20:8–12.

36. Cf. Mt 25:21.

37. Second Vatican Ecumenical Council, Pastoral Constitution on the Church in the Modern World "Gaudium et Spes," 34: AAS 58 (1966), pp. 1052–1053.

38. Ibid.

39. Second Vatican Ecumenical Council, Dogmatic Constitution on the Church "Lumen Gentium," 36: AAS 57 (1965), p. 41.

40. Mk 6:1–3.

41. Cf. Mt 13:55.

42. Cf. Mt 6:25–34.

43. Jn 15:1.

44. Cf. Sir 38:13–3.

45. Cf. Sir 38:4–8.
46. Cf. Ex 31:1–5; Sir 38:29–30.
47. Cf. Gen 4:22; Is 44:12.
48. Cf. Jer 18:3–4; Sir 38:29–30.
49. Cf. Gen 9:20; Is 5:1–2.
50. Cf. Eccles 12:9–12; Sir 39:1–8.
51. Cf. Ps 107(108):23–30: Wis 14:2–3a.
52. Cf. Gen 11:3; 2 Kings 12:12–13; 22:5–6.
53. Cf. Gen 4:21.
54. Cf. Gen 4:2; 37:3; Ex 3:1; 1 Sam 16:11; et passim.
55. Cf. Ez 47:10.
56. Cf. Prov 31:15–27.
57. E.g. Jn 10:1–16.
58. Cf. Mk 12:1–12.
59. Cf. Lk 4:23.
60. Cf. Mk 4:1–9.
61. Cf. Mt 13:52.
62. Cf. Mt 24:45; Lk 12: 42–48.
63. Cf. Lk 16:1–8.
64. Cf. Mt 13:47–50.
65. Cf. Mt 13:45–46.
66. Cf. Mt 20:1–6.
67. Cf. Mt 13:33; Lk 15:8–9.
68. Cf. Mt 9:37; Jn 4:35–38.
69. Cf. Mt 4:19.
70. Cf. Mt 13:52.
71. Cf. Acts 18:3.
72. Cf. Acts 20:34–35.
73. 2 Thess 3:8. Saint Paul recognizes that missionaries have a right to their keep. 1 Cor 9:6–14; Gal 6:6; 2 Thess 3:9; cf. Lk 10:7.
74. 2 Thess 3:12.
75. 2 Thess 3:11.
76. 2 Thess 3:10.
77. Col 3:23–24.
78. Cf. Acts 1:1.
79. Second Vatican Ecumenical Council, Pastoral Constitution on the Church in the Modern World "Gaudium et Spes," 35: AAS 58 (1966), p. 1053.
80. Ibid.
82. Gen 3:19.
83. Eccles 2:11.

84. Cf. Rom 5:19.

85. Cf. Jn 17:4.

86. Cf. Lk 9:23.

87. Second Vatican Ecumenical Council, Pastoral Constitution on the Church in the Modern World "Gaudium et Spes," 38: AAS 58 (1966), pp. 1055–1056.

88. Cf. Pt 3:13; Rev 21:1.

89. Cf. 2 Pt 3:13.

90. Second Vatican Ecumenical Council, Pastoral Constitution on the Church in the Modern World "Gaudium et Spes," 39: AAS 58 (1966), p. 1057.

91. *Ibid.*